Barnes & Noble Critical Studies

General Editor: Michael Egan

The Fiction of Sex
Themes and Functions of
Sex Difference in the Modern Novel

Barnes & Noble Critical Studies published and in preparation:

Henry James: The Ibsen Years

E. E. Cummings: A Remembrance of Miracles

Margaret Drabble: Puritanism and Permissiveness

The Silent Majority: A Study of the Working Class in Post-war British Fiction

Wyndham Lewis: Fictions and Satires

George Gissing

The Historical Novel and Popular Politics in Nineteenth-century England

The Plays of D. H. Lawrence

Reaching into the Silence: A Study of Eight Twentieth-century Visionaries

THE FICTION OF SEX

Themes and Functions of
Sex Difference in the Modern Novel

Rosalind Miles

BOOKS
10 East 53d St., New York 10022
(a division of Harper & Row Publishers, Inc.)

Barnes & Noble Books
Harper & Row, Publishers, Inc.
10 East 53rd Street
New York

ISBN 06-494822-6

For My Mother

First published in the United States, 1974

© 1974 Vision Press, London

Contents

Editorial Note

Barnes & Noble Critical Studies will examine mainly nineteenth-century and contemporary imaginative writing, delimiting an area of literary inquiry between, on the one hand, the loose generalities of the "readers' guide" approach and, on the other, the excessively particular specialist study. Crisply written and with an emphasis on fresh insights, the series will gather its coherence and direction from a broad congruity of approach on the part of its contributors. Each volume, based on sound scholarship and research, but relatively free from cumbersome scholarly apparatus, will be of interest and value to all students of the period.

M.E.E.

Acknowledgements

My thanks are due to all those who have assisted me in the writing of this book, not least those writers, living and dead, whose insights and phrases have been absorbed into my consciousness, mislaid by the delusive memory, and finally presented again delightfully to me as my own inventions.

For more tangible help I should like to thank the staff of the Birmingham Reference Library for their constant interest, courtesy, and perseverance in tracking down obscure or evasive material. I am also indebted to the library staff of the Lanchester Polytechnic for their ready co-operation and kindness.

Acknowledgements are due to the following for their kind permission to quote from copyright material: Robert Graves and A. P. Watt & Son, *The Greek Myths*; Ivy Compton-Burnett and Victor Gollancz Ltd., *Men And Wives, The Mighty And Their Fall, Brothers And Sisters, A Father And His Fate*; Iris Murdoch, Chatto & Windus Ltd., and Viking Press Inc., *The Sandcastle, The Nice And The Good, A Fairly Honourable Defeat, An Accidental Man, The Black Prince*; Mrs Katherine Jones, the Hogarth Press Ltd., and Basic Books Inc., *Sigmund Freud, Life and Work*; the estate of D. H. Lawrence by courtesy of Laurence Pollinger Ltd., *The Rainbow, Women In Love, Morality and the Novel*; Dom Moraes and Associated Book Publishers Ltd., *John Nobody*; Mary McCarthy and William Heinemann Ltd., *On The Contrary*; Leon Edel, Granada Publishing Ltd., and William Morris Agency Inc., *The Psychological Novel 1900–1950*; Hamish Hamilton Ltd., *A Perfect Woman*, copyright © L. P. Hartley, 1955; Elizabeth Jane Howard, Jonathan Cape Ltd., and Messrs A. D. Peters, *The Sea Change* and *The Long View*; Alexis Lykiard and Curtis Brown Ltd., *The Summer Ghosts*; Maureen Duffy and

Hutchinson Publishing Group Ltd., *The Single Eye*; the literary estate of Virginia Woolf, the Hogarth Press Ltd., and Harcourt Brace Jovanovich Inc., *The Death Of The Moth, A Room Of One's Own, A Writer's Diary, To The Lighthouse, The Waves*; Anthony Burgess, Faber & Faber Ltd., and Deborah Rogers Ltd., *The Novel Now*; Hazel Mews and the Athlone Press Ltd., *Frail Vessels*; Kay Dick and Duckworth Ltd., *Ivy And Stevie*; Dorothy Richardson, J. M. Dent & Sons Ltd., and Alfred A. Knopf Inc., *Pilgrimage*; Nigel Nicholson, Victoria Sackville-West's *All Passion Spent*; Quentin Bell, the Hogarth Press Ltd., and Harcourt Brace Jovanovich Inc., *Virginia Woolf: A Biography*; Doris Lessing, Curtis Brown Ltd., and Simon & Schuster Inc., *Martha Quest*; Doris Lessing, Michael Joseph Ltd., and Curtis Brown Ltd., *The Grass Is Singing* and *The Golden Notebook*; Doris Lessing, Jonathan Cape Ltd., and Curtis Brown Ltd., *Briefing For A Descent Into Hell*; Jean Rhys and André Deutsch Ltd., *I Spy A Stranger* and *Good Morning Midnight*; Barrie & Jenkins and Houghton Mifflin & Co., Carson McCullers' *The Heart Is A Lonely Hunter*; Elaine Morgan and Souvenir Press Ltd., *The Descent Of Woman*; The Bodley Head, James Joyce's *Ulysses*; the estate of Elizabeth Bowen, Jonathan Cape Ltd., and Alfred A. Knopf Inc., *The House In Paris*; Curtis Brown Ltd., Winifred Holtby's *South Riding*; E. H. Carr, Allen & Unwin Ltd., and Barnes & Noble, *Dostoevsky*; Norman Mailer and Weidenfeld Publishers Ltd., *The Prisoner of Sex*; Miss Rosamond Lehmann and the Society of Authors, *The Weather In The Streets*; Edna O'Brien and Jonathan Cape Ltd., *August Is A Wicked Month*; Margaret Drabble and Weidenfeld Publishers Ltd., *Jerusalem the Golden*; Mary McCarthy and Weidenfeld Publishers Ltd., *The Group*; Hammond Hammond, Radclyffe Hall's *A Saturday Life* and *The Well Of Loneliness*; Olwyn Hughes, Sylvia Plath's *Winter Trees*; Philip Roth, Jonathan Cape Ltd., and Random House Inc., *Portnoy's Complaint*; Anthony Burgess, William Heinemann, and W. W. Norton & Co., *A Clockwork Orange*; Beverley Gasner, Macdonald & Co. Ltd., and Brandt & Brandt, *Girls' Rules*.

To Dr Michael Egan who had faith in this book and made many invaluable suggestions, I owe a debt of gratitude; but above all my thanks go to my husband, whose help and understanding have never failed.   R.M.

1

Definitions of Sexuality

In the beginning, Eurynome, the Goddess of All Things, rose naked from Chaos, but found nothing substantial for her feet to rest upon, and therefore divided the sea from the sky, dancing lonely upon its waves. She danced towards the south, and the wind set in motion behind her seemed something new and apart with which to begin a work of creation. Wheeling about, she caught hold of this north wind, rubbed it between her hands, and behold! the great serpent Ophion. Eurynome danced to warm herself, wildly and still more wildly, until Ophion, grown lustful, coiled about those divine limbs and was moved to couple with her. Now, the North Wind, who is also called Boreas, fertilises; which is why mares often turn their hind-quarters to the wind and breed foals without aid of a stallion. So Eurynome was likewise got with child.
(Pelasgian creation myth, related by Robert Graves, *The Greek Myths*, 1955, I, 27)

Hope is woman; despair is man. (Arab proverb)

I believe women are more straightforward than men. Though they are held to be so underhand and sly. And there cannot be smoke without flame, of course.
                 (Ivy Compton-Burnett, *A Father and His Fate*, 1957, p. 7)

Sexual definition is the obligation and pastime of all cultures. Like birth, sex difference is simultaneously commonplace and esoteric, an unconsidered fact of every ordinary life and its most powerful mystery. Each society, each generation and individual, has to find a working relationship to this area of human experience, which, by constantly shifting its bounds, is constantly redefining the terms of discussion. It is not necessary to resort to anthropological and sociological cliché to show that "man" and "woman" have different meanings in different cultures; they do so between different people. The significant variations between the sexes have engrossed artists and critics throughout history; and the subject provides both the attraction and the reassurance that since this is an area where none but the simplest formal qualification is required, anyone can be an expert.

For sex definition is both a cultural and a personal activity. These are not necessarily distinct—what is called a well-integrated personality is perhaps merely one in which exterior and interior definitions correspond. Fairly frequently individual effort pulls against the current of the contemporary cultural flow; Oscar Wilde is one of society's many cautionary examples here. As his life shows, sex definition cannot be only a personal preoccupation. It is not as if the artist can come to terms with his own sex and leave it at that. Sex defines itself as much by exclusion as by any other process—male or female is not only what the "I" of any fiction is, but also what it is not. It varies too with different people, at different times. Hence the artist cannot avoid encountering sex difference as a theme, must work out its place in relation to the other ideas and observations which he wishes to convey. And as a theme, sex definition is so vast that it could hardly be overlooked. That wide expanse of human awareness and behaviour which is loosely signified by the term "sex" provides for the artist a vein so rich that it is never exhausted. Iris Murdoch's hero of *The Black Prince* (1973) protests against the subsumption of all other activities into this category which so commonly occurs:

It is customary in this age to attribute a comprehensive and quite unanalysed causality to the "sexual urges". These obscure forces, sometimes thought of as particular historical springs, sometimes as more general and universal destinies, are credited with the power to make of us, delinquents, neurotics, lunatics, fanatics, martyrs, heroes, saints, or, more exceptionally, integrated fathers, fulfilled mothers, placid human animals, and the like. Vary the mixture, and there's nothing "sex" cannot be said to explain. . .

(p. 112)

Needless to say, Bradley Pearson's protest, like his creator's conviction that we should resist classification and try instead to confront the startling singularity of every being and event, is more noted than acted upon. "Sex" has been the conditioning force of most art, supplying attitude and theme, fusing subject and object. Relationships between male and female, to take just one of its territories, constitute their own wide universe and secret world; they also provide a microcosm of the larger (real?) world outside—both these functions are well grasped by the Genesis novelist in his study of Western civilisation's first married couple, Adam and Eve. "Sex" is a living social issue, indeed a quasi-barometrical indication of any society's values will be given by its assumptions of what is appropriate sexual behaviour, the status of its women, and so on. The degenerative tendency of language, perhaps of human nature, ensures that "sex" today is all too frequently understood as "copulation"; it ought rather to stand for any aspect of behaviour which is suggested or shaped by the state of being male or female. On this standard the world of Cranford, "in possession of the Amazons" yet always needing the help of a "tame man about the house", is as full of sex activity as *Tropic of Cancer*; fuller perhaps, as showing a more developed sense of sex in its relation to every region of human activity, and not merely the horizontal.

Sex definition has in fact had a special relevance to the history and evolution of the novel. In the two hundred or so years since its decisive origination as a modern form, the novel has come to be the most popular and influential of all fictional modes, with the inevitable exception of television. Poetry and drama rapidly became and remain minority interests in comparison. From its birth the novel has shown its capacity for functioning as an agent of examination and prescription both in the realms of the immediate journalistic survey (Defoe) and of the extended metaphysical essay (Richardson). In this century at least, and probably earlier if we think no further back than Dickens, the novel has been the primary agent of the moral imagination of society. Whatever is occuring even peripherally in individual or cultural consciousness at large, we should expect to find in the novel.

Historically too the novel has been particularly well equipped to execute and transmit definitions of sex. The nineteenth-century reader turned to the novel as a listener to a tale, in the pupil relationship to the omniscient narrator. Among much that he had come to expect from the novelist was some instruction concerning the operation and interaction of character (the novel, traditionally, being "about" character). Sex, as the first known positive of character (Shakespeare's Old Shepherd in *The Winter's Tale* approaches his fostering with the basic question, "A boy or a child, I wonder?") inevitably forms a major division of the material confronting the novelist. On occasions it has constituted a gulf which he has required all the resources of his technique to bridge; and can we truly say that Dickens, for instance, with all his tremendous imaginative energy, all his reserves of satire and sentiment, of love, bluster, and despair, ever got across to the side signposted "female"?

The twentieth-century reader has been required to make a different effort. He has had to submit to being drawn into the mind of the novelist-master and taken on that interior voyage which has made up so much of recent fiction. Contemporary stress upon the importance of the individual psyche throws each writer back upon the decisive origins of his own uniqueness. Sex awareness is the first essential factor of humanity, and it is throughout life the primary imperative of being, feeling, knowing. Leon Edel, in *The Psychological Novel 1900–1950* (1955), p. ix, has referred to this "inward-turning to convey the flow of mental experience" as the single most characteristic aspect of the twentieth-century novel. Certainly we have been educated to see the confrontation of loneliness rather than the establishment of community as the business of the novel today; and as the soul casts about in search of its own self, it must encounter, somewhere in the process, that principal constituent of selfhood which is sex.

Non-literary factors have also been at work to ensure the prominence of the theme of sex differentiation in the modern novel. Much of our thinking about the distinctive characteristics of the sexes, and of women in particular, may be traced back to Freud's theories of sexual biology. Freud's linking of psychological with physiological features to produce an overall view of the female nature as weak and unable, has undergone such a fierce onslaught by feminist critics in books like Betty Friedan's *The Feminine Mystique* (1963), Kate Millett's *Sexual Politics* (1969), and Germaine Greer's *The Female Eunuch* (1970), that the observer might feel that attitudes are changing. But have we in any sense abandoned the Freudian formula? Consider his summary of the chief characteristics of the female—passivity; a fragile ego with an undeveloped sense of self; a feeble superego resulting in an underoperative conscience; the renunciation of active aims and ambitions; an incapacity for abstract thought; a retreat into inward action and fantasy. Examine *Woman's Own* and you will find this exemplified throughout.

Nor is it only at the subliterary level of fiction that the characterisation of women in these terms is carried on. Much serious work today is directed towards exposing the ironic results of such statements as this:

> I believe that all reforming action in law and education would break down in front of the fact that, long before the age at which a man can earn a position in society, Nature has determined woman's destiny through beauty, charm and sweetness. Law and custom have much to give women that has been withheld from them, but the position of women will surely be what it is: in youth an adored darling, in mature years a loved wife.
>
> (Ernest Jones, *Sigmund Freud, Life and Work*, 1953, I, 192)

The traumas of Georgy Girl, in Margaret Forster's novel of that name, of Anna in Doris Lessing's *The Golden Notebook* (1962), of most of the heroines of Jean Rhys, Mary McCarthy, and Muriel Spark, are located in the simultaneous establishment and betrayal of the unreal expectations here expressed. The big, plain, or graceless female hopelessly fails this chocolate-box beauty, charm, and sweetness test of womanhood; the deserted or divorced woman measures the extent of her loss by the magnitude of this overstrained statement of her need for protection.

To extrapolate is to distort, and this picture of Freud as a simple-minded sentimentalist does less than justice both to his reproachful self-instructions—"The loved one is not to become a toy doll, but a good comrade . . . I have been trying to smash her frankness . . ."—and to the equally genuine-sounding note of bafflement in this remark: "The great question that has never been answered and which I have not yet been able to answer, despite my thirty years of research into the feminine soul, is

15

'What does a woman want?' " (Ernest Jones, I, 122–3 and II, 468). But note the dangerously generalising assumption that there exists to be discovered a truth which will sum up and explain "a woman", all women. Despite Freud's sincerity there is an inevitable contraction and belittlement in this unconscious synecdoche, in the reduction of the entire sex to one type. Inevitably too, like all great thinkers, Freud is recalled and transmitted via a simplified outline of his teaching rather than for his full theoretical philosophy with all its qualifications. The search for the answer to Freud's "great question" goes on unabated. It is one of the staples of the twentieth-century novel.

Another historical factor which has brought sex definition to the fore as a characteristic preoccupation of the modern period is the process of the erosion of established certitudes. The theme has of course had dissimilar significance for different writers, but whether it has assumed a full centrality or lies on the edge of the created world, it can never be absent. Sometimes, indeed, writers may even succeed in imposing their own personal equations and preoccupations upon their contemporary readership; individuals have, especially in times of flux, occasionally articulated personal systems or versions of sex differentiation which have pervaded their entire culture. Something of this sort seems to have been happening in the novel of the twentieth century. In an age when so much is slipping so fast, when previously accepted forms of masculine authority like those of the church, the law, the schoolmasters, and of course the *pater familias* himself, are being questioned and repudiated, traditional sex roles are assailed but sex itself remains a constant of existence. For the uncertain it becomes the only certainty.

This is in part the explanation of the importance given to the theme by writers as diverse as D. H. Lawrence and Ernest Hemingway. The failure of the bank of common assumptions leads to the inability of writer and reader to count on the shared view; the novelist cannot begin the dialogue on the basis of shared truths already agreed. But some community of belief is implied in the successful transmission of art; consequently the modern novelist has to discover or create his own people. Up to a point this has to be a missionary activity; he who has found his truth takes it to those in darkness; and this may account for if not excuse the Messianic strain in Lawrence which is something of a trial even to his admirers. But these writers' assertion of masculinity in terms of supremacy not only over women but over all other animals, difficulties, and setbacks, must be seen against the background of their period. In the difficult decades following the First World War, those men who survived that holocaust had to face another test, in the changed world that confronted them. They were under a variety of pressures to examine and exert themselves, but at the same time found that various formerly accepted modes of masculine behaviour—father, husband, soldier, lover—were never again to mean what they had meant before. Small wonder then that *cojones*, in Hemingway's evocative term, seemed to emerge as the ultimate standard; here, at least, was something a man could hold on to.

D. H. Lawrence has been a key figure in twentieth-century attempts at sex definition. He himself drew attention to the primacy of this theme in his thinking:

> The great relationship, for humanity, will always be the relation between man and woman. The relation between man and man, woman and woman, parent and child, will always be subsidiary.
>
> And the relation between man and woman will change for ever, and will be the new central clue to human life.

("Morality and the Novel", *Calendar of Modern Letters*, December 1925)

This intense conviction never left him. It is not the least of the tributes to his powers that he was able to create a similar conviction in the minds of so many others. In trying to describe what he saw and felt, in seeking to render scrupulously what to him was literal truth, Lawrence articulated one of the most potent myths of our time, that of the fundamental and irreconcilable opposition of male and female. It is unjust to attribute all the excesses of the cult of advanced bullhood to Lawrence. It is at least arguable that his contribution was to posit the primitive loneliness of the soul as wandering in the void between male and female. But so often in Lawrence's fiction, with only a slight shift of perspective the void becomes a minefield dividing the sexes, a state of hostilities is assumed though not always declared, and it is enjoined upon the participants to stand and defend themselves how they will. Inevitably the positions adopted in a war situation are extreme; loyalties become polarised and competition supersedes co-operation:

> His eyes grew round, he did not know where he was. How could she, his own wife, say such a thing? But she sat there, small and foreign and separate. It dawned on him she did not consider herself his wife, except in so far as they agreed. She did not feel she had married him. At any rate, she was willing to allow he might want another woman. A gap, a space opened before him.
>
> (*The Rainbow*, 1915, Chapter III)

Generations of the uncertain have turned to Lawrence for his handling of moments like this. He seems to offer unique glimpses into the heart of the matter, rare flashes of perception of the genuine state of relationships between female and male. Many of his readers have found reassurance if not certainty in Lawrence's treatment of the man's role in sex relations. It has been and is widely taken as offering a new form of authority and power to replace the older social and political means by which man declared and supported his supremacy. Lawrence himself never says anything as simple as this; but his work typically suffers distortions in transmission. All his subtleties, refinements, qualifications are lost as a handful of phrases, ideas, scenes are abstracted and disseminated—not for nothing has he been called a "seminal" writer. And Lawrence himself clouded his utterance not only by his liking for pseudognomic and would-be reverberant obscurities, but also by his reliance upon some quite ineffably drivelling notions of human behaviour and needs (see Frank Kermode's *Lawrence*, 1973, for an unduly uncritical exegesis of some hysterical and dangerous theories which in a lesser man would have been plainly recognised as lunatic).

Most of Lawrence's follies have perished now, and lie in an obscurity from which we wrong him to rescue them. But one of his most damaging concepts has proved enormously influential. Even in his best fiction Lawrence never overcame a deep anti-feminism, which is manifested in various ways. First, there are the overt attacks upon female characters, with the suggestion that they contain a truth about woman's nature in general. He repeatedly asserts that his ideal of the "freedom in love" of "two pure beings" is spoiled by the female instinct to turn love into "a worship of perfect possession":

> But it seemed to him, woman was always so horrible and clutching, she had such a lust for possession, a greed of self-importance in love. She wanted to have, to own, to control, to be dominant. Everything must be referred back to her, to Woman, the Great Mother of everything out of whom proceeded everything and to whom everything must finally be rendered up.
>
> (*Women In Love*, 1921, Chapter XVI)

Then there is the constant use in the novels of women characters merely as agents in the growth and career of a man, rather than as individuals in their own right; for they have no individual right, in that sense, in Lawrence's eyes. Birkin makes this point via a grossly unflattering comparison:

> "And woman is the same as horses: two wills act in opposition inside her. With one will, she wants to subject herself utterly. With the other, she wants to bolt, and pitch her rider to perdition."
>
> "Then I'm a bolter," said Ursula, with a burst of laughter.
>
> 'It's a dangerous thing to domesticate even horses, let alone women," said Birkin. "The dominant principle has some rare antagonists."
>
> "Good thing too," said Ursula.
>
> "Quite," said Gerald with a faint smile. "There's more fun."
>
> (*Women In Love*, Chapter XII)

Notice that a woman here is seen only and entirely in the context of her "rider". There is in this sequence, which follows the episode of Gerald's torturing the mare, a sadism which is not even latent. With such attitudes, these men turn love into an insulting denial of their partner's womanhood and real self. Birkin makes his conditions clear to Ursula thus: "I don't *want* to see you. I've seen plenty of women, I'm sick and weary of seeing them. I want a woman I don't see." Again: "I want to find you, where you don't know your own existence, the you that your common self denies utterly. But I don't want your good looks, and I don't want your womanly feelings, and I don't want your thoughts nor opinions nor your ideas—they are all bagatelles to me." When Ursula protests at this, he dismisses her complaints as "meretricious persiflage". So although he refines his offer as "an equilibrium, a pure balance of two single beings:—as the stars balance each other" we see that the question of her equality in it is absurd. This is later reinforced by Lawrence when he shows us Birkin's tomcat demonstrating his superiority over a female cat by cuffing her. Ursula's disapproval draws on her the contempt of master and beast. Again, as with Gerald, her feminism is made to appear petulant and ridiculous, exercised as it is in defence of animals. So many of Lawrence's studies of women are subtly reductive in this way, trivialising their actions and concerns. And so much is conveyed, too, by the deployment of the unacknowledged generalisation. For despite the very marked surface dissimilarities between his female characters, which have given him the largely undeserved reputation of being expert in the mysteries of woman's nature, all Lawrence's women suffer from the same complaint in differing degrees: "will", the "darkness in the blood', and dreams of dominance.

Lawrence's personal conduct has also had a measurable effect upon the establishing of twentieth-century ideas of sexuality. He approached the whole business in a crusading spirit, and not only through the dramas of his less-than-private life do we see the knight-errant at work. Most of his life was a continuous effort to live his own philosophy and to get others to do so too. His attempts to influence the relationships of those he encountered according to his theories can be seen in his fictional revenges on those who failed to accept his direction; Compton Mackenzie considered a writ over *The Man Who Loved Islands*, and Katherine Mansfield and Middleton Murry found it almost inconceivable when they learned that they had served as models for Gudrun and Gerald in *Women In Love*. There are several other such examples.

Yet all this, paradoxically, has enhanced rather than diminished his reputation as a great contemporary seer and prophet. Lawrence has been interpreted by many as a man who spoke and wrote from a far wider sexual experience than they would ever have, and who, at whatever cost to others or to himself, like Ibsen's Brand, practised what he preached. Like Freud, Lawrence has been remembered and transmitted rather in terms of a readily digestible version of his ideas than through the dark maze of his complex world picture. And so, by a process which lies midway between the intensification natural to art and the simplification inherent in popularisation, the formula, the Lawrentian formula, has been evolved. Sex relations constitute a struggle for mastery, which the man must win, for the psychic health of the woman as much as for his own. Women, dark and dangerous, need "phallic hunting out"; they need a man, but will, through innate inferiority and the envy that that produces, almost invariably damage and fail him.

Whatever a distant posterity pronounces upon Lawrence, when the dust that he raised in his lifetime finally settles, there can be little point in denying him his place in contemporary literary history. It is fair to say that he was the first novelist to achieve a specifically and exclusively sexual focus in his presentation of female character; he began the intense interest in women's sexual emotions and needs which has burgeoned in our time into a little sub-species of the novel of its own. Bernard Bergonzi, in *The Situation of the Novel* (1970), Chapter I, has pointed with some reservations to the fragmentation of the novel today into "genres", particularly that concerning "a very sensitive, rather neurotic girl . . . having sexual difficulties—conventional, or lesbian, or both". This Bergonzi interprets as a diminishing if not a cessation of its former growth. The appearance and continued popularity of this type of "woman's novel" may be laid at Lawrence's door. As with Freud, we see again how easily the shocking and hard-won definitions of one generation become the models and stereotypes of the next.

Of course the recognition and discussion of women's sexual needs which we owe to Freud and Lawrence in chief, was a tremendous liberation for both sexes from the manifold and deforming constrictions of the nineteenth century. But it has, with a deep irony, become the new tyranny. It sometimes seems as if women cannot be studied in fiction now except in terms of their sexual emotions, often interpreted unflatteringly; the unacknowledged urges, the will to harm, the masochistic search for the man who will dominate. Even so chic and up-to-the-minute a trifle as Muriel Spark's *The Driver's Seat* (1970) conforms to this outline in every particular. Strip away the modish accessories with which Muriel Spark delights to equip her characters—the pine-lined flat, the intercontinental flights, the luxury hotels and hired cars—and this novel, which has been hailed as a stylish

21

allegory, is seen as yet another picture of a dim and deadly female with a massive neurosis due to shortage of sex, who flies to Italy, home of Latin lovers, determined to do and die.

As this suggests, the effects of the Lawrentian formula have been just as potent upon women writers as upon men. It is not simply a myth operative upon adolescent males, and mercifully outgrown in maturity, like acne. It has defined for men and women of all ages what seemed to be a commanding and imaginative version of sex relations. Women have studied themselves in Lawrence's terms, accepting his basic notions as authority—a parallel might be sought with the position in psychology which the Freudian view of women has held so unassailably for so long, with women psychoanalysts like Helene Deutsch enthusiastically endorsing the antifeminist work of their male colleagues. Certainly it is to be found that there is even now a remarkable lack of interest among women writers (and men too) in the subject of women's work, unless it be the atypical domestic routine of the child-bound Ph.D. Admittedly the life of a biscuit-packer, typist, or char, may lack allure, but it is surely significant that there has been no female equivalent of *Saturday Night And Sunday Morning* (1958) or *A Kind Of Loving* (1960), both of which treat the slow disabling of the (masculine) soul through boring repetitive labour. With some exceptions it is still alarmingly axiomatic even in serious fiction that love is "woman's whole existence" and that human relationships are the *real* work of a women's life. Twentieth-century literature shows no more sign of rejecting the Lawrentian formula than the Freudian; indeed psychology and literature have combined to offer a doctrine which is now become dogma.

Lawrence's repeated stress on the secret and primitive nature of sex difference has perhaps been his most important single legacy. Both men and women writers since have been straining every nerve to capture the difference and set it down. Sexual definition has become something between a fine art and a neurosis in the novel of the second half of the twentieth century. Ironically, in a world which many feel offers more prospect of equality and justice to each individual than at any historical moment previously, male and female are in fact (and in fiction) emotionally drawing apart. Sexual definition has come to mean for many writers a convulsive effort of separation, of division. To this we owe that ten-

22

sion between the sexes which must accompany any heightened awareness of these differences. Clearly this is not the discovery of the modern period alone. *Lysistrata* turns as closely on the theme as *The Way Of The World* does. The ancient world also amply illustrates too that fear of women which expresses itself as antifeminism or through various propitiatory devices— Medusa, Clytemnestra, the Erinnyes who hounded the taboo-breaker to a terrible death, all were aspects of the female, just as much as Penelope or poor Iphigenia, the eternal victim.

All cultures will afford many such examples of the tradition of hostility if not downright antipathy between the sexes. But the modern emphasis upon sex differentiation has put a new edge on the old blade. Fresh insights into sex difference increase polarisation of attitudes. Female emancipation may not have freed all women from their historic servitude to traditional concepts, but it has helped to awaken their consciousness of it; even one of the more privileged of her sex could write with the latent bitterness which always marked her comments on the subject: "Women have served all these centuries as looking-glasses possessing the magic and delicious power of reflecting the figure of man at twice its natural size" (Virginia Woolf, *A Room Of One's Own*, 1929, p. 53). A modern poet has summed up the contemporary situation (notice how the poem's form is as much as ironic parody of older modes as is its content):

> My friend the poet often thinks of women
> But has become, by use, remote and wary.
> Though he has found them in the past inhuman
> He does not cease to find them necessary.
>
> So from his papers he looks up much haunted
> By dreams of lacewrapped breasts and nylon thighs,
> And going out, finds a girl who always wanted
> Somebody brainy, and who likes his eyes.
>
> They wrestle by her bed, till a detected
> Faint flash, in the madonna face, of malice
> Shakes him: like one who fears to be infected
> He hesitates above her, then, instead,
> Doing up his trousers, flusters through black alleys
> Back to where papers fail to warm his bed.

(Dom Moraes, *John Nobody*, 1965, p. 15)

23

Suspicion, tension, inadequacy, failure—is this too gloomy a picture of the state of sex relations as a result of sexual definition in the twentieth century?

We have so far considered male and female simply as the two basic groupings of the human race. What is perhaps more important to literature is not the question of the possession of one sex or another, which can usually be demonstrated. Of greater significance in art and perhaps also in life has been the use of male and female as symbols or abstracts of opposed or complementary qualities. Mary Ellman, in *Thinking About Women* (1968), has shown how assumptions as to the nature of male and female condition the formulation of all ideas, and not only those relating to the human species itself. Each sex is taken as representing a certain complex of values, and anything which resembles or approximates to either becomes, by extension, "male" or "female". Hence "all imagined forms of fear and punishment, like God and the Devil, are masculine. So are those aggressive powers, the sun and the wind" (p. 9). To the female forces are reserved the rights of making trouble, the Lilith syndrome. Even the mental processes themselves are subject to this simplification—"By sexual correlation, all energy or enterprise is customarily assigned to male thought, and simple, accretive expectation to female thought" (p. 13). It is widely assumed that men and women write differently and even think differently, because they are enforced to live differently in certain basic ways, that there is between men and women a profound difference of intellect both in quantity and quality analogous to the significant physical variations between the sexes. This is not only a masculine prejudice operating to the disadvantage of women. Virginia Woolf observed of Middleton Murry (who seems often to have had this effect on women, even upon those who loved him), "I think what an abrupt precipice cleaves asunder the male intelligence, and how they pride themselves upon a point of view which much resembles stupidity". It should be observed that these impressions persist only in the Western version of our Judæo-Christian inheritance, and are inapplicable to, say, the Hellenistic experience. But all cultures, all story-tellers, all writers and thinkers depend upon sexual analogy; even a boat has to have a sex projected on to it:

24

"ships are compartmental and hollow, ships are like women" (*The Black Prince*, p. 81).

Male and female also represent, to some extent, different modes of writing, whether critical or creative. Mary Ellman has attempted to analyse sex difference as expressed through difference of tone between men and women writers (Chapter IV, pp. 148–174). She argues that the "male" mode contains and conveys authority, weight, rationality, knowledge, and control. By opposition the "female" mode is intuitive, formless, subtle, over-intense ("shrill" is the word used to derogate this quality in women's writing). Ellman sees this as a false dichotomy, originating early in the nineteenth century when women first began to publish not only as novelists but as what we now call "intellectuals". This provoked in consequence a male response which codified its own utterance in the more commanding terms both in definition and in defence. This opposition tends to stereotype production; some women "repeat the ritual gestures of sensibility, just as some men repeat those of authority", and never find their own voice. We could add that these modes are not necessarily adopted according to sex. Many women writers, especially in the nineteenth century, sought and achieved the masculine mode, and its stylistic corre- lative, the rhetorical stance. Similarly many men have tried to avoid the external view, the public posture that this implies, and have chosen instead the equivocations of irony, the interior dialogue, the subjective flow. This is discussed at length in Lisa Appignanesi's *Femininity and the Creative Imagination* (1973). She sums up part of her argument as follows:

> Feminine, then, as a term of literary description would suggest an art of which the two distinguishing features are interiorisation and the conscious creation of mystery either around or within the work of art. The long historical insistence on the otherness of woman, her core of feminine mystery, makes her the natural focus for an art which finds no fruitful material in what it considers the prose of ordinary life and which seeks to transcend the configura- tions of a known reality.

> (p.15)

Again, broad concepts of masculine and feminine underlie and determine critical attitudes, providing not only the orientation but also the imagery. So D. S. Savage writes of Hemingway that

25

his values are a "product of the battlefield", and of Virginia Woolf: "The distinguishing feature of Virginia Woolf's apprehension of life lies precisely in its passivity . . . it is a typical feature of the characters in her novels to be altogether lacking in the capacity for discriminating within experience. They are passively caught up in the stream of events, of 'life', of their own random perceptions" (*The Withered Branch*, 1950, p. 95). A perfectly "feminine" picture, in fact, both of author and characters. Virginia Woolf, with a rather dating coyness, herself said "Fiction is a lady, and a lady who has somehow got herself into trouble"; this metaphor has been updated by Norman Mailer in his (rhetorical?) claim that the novel is the Great Bitch; writing is dominating her sexually, good writing is "making her squeal". We hear it said as a term of approbation, and signifying its effectiveness, that a certain novel or piece of prose "rapes the sensibilities". This use of male and female to delineate (or, as here, to expropriate) areas of activity or sensibility in literature is a standard practice. Consider the following reflections on the contemporary novel by Mary McCarthy:

> The fictional experiments of the twentieth century went in two directions: sensibility and sensation. To speak very broadly, the experiments in the recording of sensibility were made in England (Virginia Woolf, Katherine Mansfield, Dorothy Richardson, Elizabeth Bowen, Forster), and America was the laboratory of sensation (Hemingway and his imitators, Dos Passos, Farrell). The novel of sensibility was feminine, and the novel of sensation was masculine. . . . The effect of these two tendencies on the subject matter of the novel was identical. Sensation and sensibility are the poles of each other, and both have the effect of abolishing the social. Sensibility, like violent action, annihilates the sense of character.
>
> (*On The Contrary*, 1962, pp. 275–6)

The novel here is seen as doing what every individual artist must do, that is, coming to terms with those areas of experience which we find in apposition within ourselves and call male and female. The artist as hermaphrodite matches himself against the hermaphroditic potential of this most subtle and flexible of fictional forms. But equally interesting here in McCarthy's comment is the illustration of how easy it is even for an intelligent and highly critical woman to accept unquestioned the rationalisations of male commentators, how difficult to resist the unfelt tyranny of modern sexual stereotypes. So the passive role, feeling, is feminine, while doing, being assertive, is masculine. A similar apposition is made by R. L. Stevenson of life and art. There is no end to the versatility of sexual analogy:

> Life is monstrous, infinite, illogical, abrupt, and poignant; a work of art in comparison is neat, finite, self-contained, rational, flowing and emasculate. Life imposes by brute energy, like inarticulate thunder; catches the ear, among the louder noises of experience, like an air artificially made by a discreet musician. . . .
>
> (Leon Edel, p. 23)

The analogy is not quite perfect here. We cannot allow, so late in the day, any disturbance of the received view of informed sources, that the analytical faculty, indeed all rational capacity, is a masculine prerogative. Femininity represents and expresses all the interior and inward-turning mental processes; it should not ask for anything more.

But who says so? Who are the opinion-makers whose views colour those of us all? It can hardly be stated too often that these definitions are all the product of a male-dominated culture, all fashioned according to masculine habits of mind. The occasional critic who is female (and women like Charlotte Lennox and Elizabeth Inchbald have been making their contribution to criticism for centuries) can have little effect upon the views of a society where all forms of authority, and all media of communication, are in the hands of men. Is it any wonder, then, that all accounts of masculine and feminine are so masculine-oriented, with all the vital powers of the mind and the shaping instincts reserved to the male, described as "masculine" even when occurring in a woman. These terms, with the inevitable if unconscious belittling of the female which is implied, fail totally to do justice to that half of the human race whose interests are nominally represented under the heading "feminine". There has been no attempt to understand the creative process in women artists as something *sui generis*. This may well be because it is only so recently in the history of human evolution that women have been trying to speak in their own voices, publish under their own names, tell it from within. At all events these concepts of "masculine" and "feminine" have

27

been imposed on one half of the species by the other, however willingly women have endorsed them, and need to be replaced by some that could be said to command a general acceptance.

Another objection to the use of these terms must be their imprecision. Either can mean anything that the speaker wishes. Lisa Appignanesi has drawn attention to the overlapping and confusion which are inescapable adjuncts to the use of the concept:

> Literary critics repeatedly use the word "feminine" to describe a writer, his vision, or his characters. It is often suggested that Henry James and Marcel Proust are "feminine" writers, in contrast to the purely masculine Hemingway. Though George Eliot is personally said to have a strong "masculine" side, yet her male characters are thought to be "too feminine". Wedekind's Lulu, Strindberg's Miss Julie, or Norman Mailer's "Great Bitch" are all quoted as being embodiments of the "feminine" principle. So too, somewhat paradoxically, are Dostoievsky's golden-hearted whore, Sonya, in *Crime and Punishment* and Joyce's faithful-faithless Molly Bloom.
>
> (p. 1)

This confusion is neatly illustrated by the following remorselessly circular dialogue from Ivy Compton-Burnett's *The Mighty And Their Fall* (1961):

> "Teresa writes like a man," said Egbert, looking at the letter.
> "I have noticed that," said Selina. "I have thought her a little like a man in herself."
> "I should have said she was the pure feminine," said Lavinia. "Herself and all to do with her. I don't remember her writing. I don't mean anything against her."
> "Why should you?" said Ninian. "What are you but feminine yourself?"
> "Oh, not purely, Father. Either in myself or as I have been influenced. It is quite a different thing."
> "Well, something is different."
> "We think of masculine women as tall and strong," said Egbert. "Teresa is neither."
> "I did not mean masculine in that sense," said Selina.

As this suggests, the use of these words places the speaker in the position of one throwing a rope across a chasm and vainly hoping

28

that it will hold. Each speaker here uses the terms to mean "What I am not", "What I disapprove of", or "What I feel exists as a quantity or entity but which I am under no obligation to link with the sex whose name I have called it by". Each of the characters is also possessed by a patent assurance of his or her own uniqueness and superiority to conventional sex typing. Possibly this is something common to us all; in the grip of what Iris Murdoch has called the "fat relentless ego" we feel only our own dazzling particularity, and readily resort to the comfort of generalisation when it comes to any other, especially the other sex. Who has not been guilty of some assumption like that of Cranford's Miss Pole: "My father was a man, and I know the sex pretty well"?

The critic who takes on this pervasive and only half-conscious process of the generalised use of these terms finds himself striking at shadows. When challenged, nobody uses these passwords. "Masculine" and "Feminine" may stand for such and such, or then again, they may not. The baffled may take refuge in Ninian's cautious platitude quoted above: "Something is different." It seems that what we call by these words are really names for the complementary functions of the personality which are not specifically or even necessarily related to physical sex difference. Strong, weak, aggressive, submissive, analytical, intuitive; these are all ways of being, of behaving, which all people, regardless of sex, are potentially capable of.

It would seem to be time for criticism to abandon the use of these terms, which are not only inadequate but tendentious. If we assume the existence of "masculine" and "feminine" then we must accept by logical extension that each should be largely if not wholly seen in the sex whose name it carries. But can it in any way be shown that the intelligences of male and female function differently? Do creative men and women actually think and write differently? Could we draw up a plausible check-list of the qualities of both sexes as expressed in and through literature?

Female	Male
Sensitivity	Brutality
Precision: words as decoration	Scope: words as tools
Insight into relationships	Analysis of structures
Perception of detail	Sense of the grand design

Social observation	Moral awareness
Slave mentality: manipulative skills	Arrogance: ability to dominate
	Aggression/"masculine perswasive force"
Submission/resignation	
Intuition	Intelligence
Subjectivity	Objectivity
Involvement	Detachment
Irony	Honesty

Clearly not. Once the list is drawn up in this way, the manifold injustices and absurdities of sex-based criticism plainly appear; it is as unfair to Hardy to deny him his irony as it is to Charlotte Brontë to suggest that her aggression is inappropriate to her.

There are other ways, too, of showing the irrelevance of sex-typing in a critical response to literature. Who could say with confidence which of these passages was written by a male and which by a female novelist?

The sense of spiritual expansion, which she once used to have, came back to her; the hard core, the feeling of a centrifugal force at work in her, contracting her—her will, she thought it was, her will, forcing her nature against its grain—began to loosen and dissolve, to be replaced by a soft pliancy of being, receptive not rebellious. The shadow stalking at her side made her feel taller than she was. Ah, here was something she liked better than the villas: the long plain Georgian façade of the convent, a white oblong against the parti-coloured hill-side. Why did she like it better than the villas? Because it spoke of an unmixed resolve, a single-minded wish to serve—she didn't trouble to ask whom; the wish to serve, the self lost in serving, was sufficient.

But alone, her happiness, the extraordinary peace of mind which had been hers when he had gone, seemed now to have dwindled to a little painful pin point of anxiety, to which, however restless her mind, she seemed fastened. No thought matched with any other: she felt bereft, and she did not know why; she felt sadly isolated from everybody else in the house, and yet she did not want to be with any one of them; she wanted this long, empty day to be finished, but had no desire for the next one; she could no longer bear to remember minutely the evening ride after the storm, and yet she was terrified of forgetting any moment of it. She felt exhausted—wasted, and sleep seemed not only more exhaustion, further waste, but impossible. Burning, shivering, from these irre-

30

concilable longings and rejections of longings she lay, until, just before her thoughts ran down to sleep, she wondered how all the countless people who must have felt as she was now feeling had managed to bear it.

What both passages here illustrate in their different ways are similarly conventional views of woman's nature and behaviour. The "she" of the first is experiencing the Lawrentian difficulty over "will," which is alien to her "true" nature, a constricting or damaging force. How well do students of sex differentiation recognise the type of female excellence referred to as "a soft pliancy of being"; how familiar is the slackness and diffuseness here expressed, as a common manifestation of what occurs in a sex where drive and potency are usually socially inhibited. Significant too is the woman's sense of her own insignificance; she walks tall only in her own shadow. Her attraction to the "long plain" white convent suggests the innate Puritanism of the undeveloped female, while another traditional female attribute is suggested in the last sentence; although the character in the novel is not masochistic or self-sacrificing, she is residually "female" enough to be compelled by the idea of "the self lost in serving".

The second passage gives us an equally stereotyped picture of the effects of love on a young woman. Her awareness of her lover is represented by the ludicrously belittling image of the pimple of anxiety. Her mental processes are totally dislocated, as is her contact with her family; her secret emotions drain her daily life of all colour and meaning. Yet she can impose no order on her memories of the love experience; oscillating between extremes, she is a prey to that common female complaint which in a less flattering context Mr Bennet describes as his wife's "nerves". The final impression of the paragraph reinforces what has been implied throughout, the impression of the woman as a delicate and precariously-articulated instrument, emotionally unstable, mentally insecure, and only just able to withstand life's buffetings.

This effect can be reproduced many times over. Consider, in contrast, the following two passages, again with a view to deducing the writer's sex from the material:

Lying in the foetus position, I turned my back on her, although she reached out towards me. I couldn't have got a peep out of the

31

old man that night. Feeling her hand on my loins, I pretended to be asleep and she turned away and satisfied herself. Often she wanted me to take her from behind, working away to make sure she came, two animals in a rut, and because it was easier it often happened like that. So tonight, I thought, didn't make any real difference, though a kind of slow resentment began to build in me, not that I minded because she was a woman, as Lawrence's game-keeper bloke would have, but because it meant complete divorce, there was no us there.

I awoke first, and as I looked at her sleeping face with its gar-lands of dark hair, felt the aching desire to weld our bodies to-gether. I roused her only when I entered her, and her drowsy moan increased my sensuality, rendering me still more ruthless in our lovemaking—penis a metronome, the plunging strokes our only gauge of time's bureaucratic dominion. Then we slid into a slow hypnotic rhythm. I levered myself up on my elbows, stretching my feet, so that we were connected, she and I, only by our genitals. Then I subsided. We clasped each other tighter than before, grind-ing our bodies together, crushing. . . .

As before what we have here are not the easily distinguished products of male and female, but two attempts to achieve a recognis-able male mode, though the first treats the frustration of out-going love and the second is more preoccupied with the flattering and satisfying of the consuming self. The first affects a vulgarian tone, presumably to lend authenticity to the narrative, with much reliance on slang, joky masculine euphemism ("the old man"), and the man-to-man approach ("not that I minded", "bloke"). Also firmly present, despite the direct disclaimer of Lawrentian attitudes, is the ghost of Lawrence himself, not only in the phras-ing ("loins"), but also very much in the disapproval of the woman's reservation of the initiative in sexual activity, and in the expecta-tion that the union should be an assertion of "us".

The second extract essays the mode poetical, which it captures so perfectly as to attain, bar one or two phrases, the heights of a woman's magazine piece. Here the writer projects himself not as the unassuming (almost unlettered) ordinary "bloke" of the first, but as a creative sexual athlete. Despite the unvaryingly self-delighted tone, there is an uneasy alternation between the pseudo-lyrical sub-Keatsian phraseology ("garlands", "drowsy moan"), and the unconsciously absurd subject-matter ("I levered myself up on my elbows", "grinding our bodies together"). Note too the modish suggestion of brutality thrown in, the "ruthless" sensuality, the "crushing" and "grinding". But are these extracts so written as to give any indication of the sex of the writer? Can one deduce a masculine controlling intelligence either from the subtle anti-feminism of the first, with its sense of the woman as a harsh greedy foreign creature, or from the second, because of its consistent (if consistently inappropriate) use of imagery drawn from the world of machines and instruments (the "masculine" world)? It is arguable that all that can be clearly seen in these two pieces is the confirmation of the fact that it is virtually impossible to find the tone and vocabulary appropriate to a successful description of sexual intercourse, no matter what sex you are.[1]

Do men and women write differently from one another? Of course they do; but from one another as individuals rather than as sexes. All writers who can claim the title write differently, that is all. Surely the time has come for criticism and literature to be released from the tyranny of the unbudging sexual stereotype. This suggestion is hardly new or original. Several writers have made it their life's work to explore and establish the inter-sexuality of much human behaviour through the discovery of the unsuspected fullness of the individual consciousness. James Joyce is the first in this field, but he shares the fate of most of the greatest geniuses, and certainly of all great linguistic experimentalists, of proving to be a literary dead end; in the long run, the novel sunk under him. Other writers in their own lives have shown how easily the sexual roles overlap; Scott Fitzgerald knew that his wife Zelda looked on him as the woman in the partnership, but he nevertheless regarded her as his child. In her adolescence Katherine Mansfield wrote "I am a child, a woman, and more than half man"; in her increasingly dreadful last years the man in her took over, perhaps driven to it by the failure of the man in Middleton Murry to do any such thing, and she sum-

[1] The first extract is from L. P. Hartley's *A Perfect Woman* (1955), Chapter 25. The second comes from Elizabeth Jane Howard's *The Long View* (1956), Part Five, Chapter 4. The third is by Maureen Duffy, *The Single Eye* (1964), Part Two, and the fourth is taken from Alexis Lykiard's *The Summer Ghosts* (1964), Chapter III.

moned her woman friend "L.M." to her side with the words "I do love you and want you for my wife".[2]

Of course, common usage of the terms "masculine" and "feminine" is not the result of any conscious critical activity in the minds of those who employ them. What they describe are socially-directed sexual responses, descriptions of personalities cultured into complementary action. This in itself makes for territorial awareness in delineating male and female; both sexes display an uneasy half-consciousness that the areas of behaviour must be kept distinct in the service of some dim notion of the health of society. We must allow too for the constant and pervasive processes of sexual analogy. From this we find that male characters are presented and judged according to a set of criteria which includes strength, resource, initiative, while for women the prescription includes a greater degree of fragility, dependence, conventionality, and reliance upon external supports.

As we have seen, both male and female writers unite to support these social clichés of behaviour. In this way externally imposed patterns pass for sexual definitions informed by personal experience. Since the management of society has been largely in the hands of men, there is a case to be made out for regarding women as the products of men's imagination, conceived and shaped by men, the cultural a reversal of the biological sequence. A nineteenth-century novelist and feminist, Olive Schreiner, remarked from bitter personal discovery in her essay on *Woman and Labour* (1911), that "we all enter the world little plastic beings, with so much natural force, perhaps, but for the rest—blank; and the world tells us what we are to be, and shapes us by the ends it sets before us".

It is very probable that for most people the conventional sex definitions are not inexact. They are also probably useful and not harmful in many areas of life. But the artist is not like common men. He or she is the most protean of creatures, and must rightly command a bisexuality or at least ambivalence of approach to

[2] Nancy Milford, in *Zelda Fitzgerald: A Biography* (1970) describes these aspects of the Fitzgeralds' relationship on pages 261 and 308. Katherine Mansfield's remarks are recorded in her *Journal*, edited by J. Middleton Murry (1954), p. 13, and in *Katherine Mansfield: The Memories of L.M.* (1971), p. 203.

life and art if he is to be capable of bodying out for us forms and themes beyond our comprehension. How familiar we are with the repeated cant about the modern artist breaking new ground, establishing new boundaries, aided and applauded by the "new" criticism! How strange is it then that both art and criticism continue to cling to the inherited constriction of nineteenth-century sexual definition, the rigid stereotypes of male and female!

2

Creativity and Sex

My profession is literature; and in that profession there are fewer experiences for women than in any other, with the exception of the stage—fewer, I mean, that are peculiar to women. For the road was cut many years ago—by Fanny Burney, by Aphra Behn, by Harriet Martineau, by Jane Austen, by George Eliot—many famous women, and many more unknown and forgotten, have been before me, making the path smooth, and regulating my steps. Thus, when I came to write, there were very few material obstacles in my way. Writing was reputable and harmless occupation. The family peace was not broken by the scratching of a pen. No demand was made on the family purse. For ten and sixpence one can buy paper enough to write all the plays of Shakespeare—if one has a mind that way. Pianos and models, Paris, Vienna and Berlin, masters and mistresses, are not needed by a writer. The cheapness of writing paper is, of course, the reason why women have succeeded as writers before they have succeeded in other professions.

(Virginia Woolf, "Professions for Women", *The Death Of The Moth*, 1942, p. 149)

The question of sex difference has had a peculiar relevance to the novel throughout its history. We have so far considered the fictional significance of the difference between male and female, and the use of these abstracts as symbols of or critical approximations to certain modes. In another direction, sex difference has influenced the novel in a way that it has not affected other art forms. Sex is a basic division of artists, and the novel is the only art form in which women have participated in numbers large enough to make their presence felt, or to which they have contributed on anything like equal terms with men. It has been the preferred form for women writers almost since women began to write, and it has in recent years been the medium through which women have investigated and publicised those aspects of their life as sexual beings which have not previously been acknowledged by art or society.

When we say "women writers", though, we mean "women novelists". However the fact is explained in terms of culturation, women have so far been unable to make any very noticeable contribution to any other literary form. This is not intended as an aspersion upon the stature of individual women poets or dramatists. On the contrary, it must surely throw into relief the poetic achievement of Emily Brontë that we can find so few other women even to place on the steps of her pedestal. Elizabeth Barrett Browning, Christina Rossetti, Emily Dickinson, Edith Sitwell, Anne Sexton, Sylvia Plath, all rise to mind—but can the list in all honesty be taken much further? Inga-Stina Ewbank makes this point in her study of the Brontë sisters, *Their Proper Sphere* (1966), p. 155: "Whether she was a perfect woman or not, the art of Emily Brontë makes us see that there is an order of creative genius where the sex of the possessor ceases to matter. The only vital 'woman question' in her case is: why are there no women poets like her?"

There are indeed a whole series of problems for the critic in the fact of Emily Brontë's virtually unique position in literature as a woman poet. It is sometimes assumed that women writers will take to writing poetry when they have outgrown their historical handicap of being "late starters" and manage to catch up with men. Virginia Woolf thought this way; she saw the woman novelist as the woman artist in embryo. Female writing she thought of as necessarily evolving in the direction of poetry, and the woman writer as needing only some traditionally masculine privileges and freedoms to enable her to make up the distance between the male and female accomplishment. In 1929 she wrote:

> Give her another hundred years . . . give her a room of her own and five hundred a year, let her speak her mind and leave out half that she now puts in, and she will write a better book one of these days. She will be a poet . . . in another hundred years' time.

> (*A Room Of One's Own*, p. 142)

37

But this seems to be founded on a variety of dubious premises. Should we take it that poetry is unquestionably of a higher order in literature than novel-writing, because it predates it as a form? Are all other writers poets at heart, poets manqué, longing like Don Armado in *Love's Labour's Lost* to "turn sonnet", as the clown is supposed to nurse aspirations to play Hamlet? Again, there are no logical grounds for assuming that the woman novelist is a poet *in potentia*, like the Alchemist's base metals which "would be gold if they had time". Even if we accept the evolutionary theory of literature, the notion that the novel is developing towards poetry is historically fallacious, as reversing the assumed "flow". Nor is it necessarily true that the novel and the poem are contiguous forms. Few writers have attempted both, and fewer still have succeeded in both; who would discover Hardy or Lawrence as poets if they did not first encounter them as writers of prose? There can be no doubt as to which of the forms these writers excel in; we could even ask, who would in fact ever read the poetry of Hardy and Lawrence but for the light it sheds on the novels and short stories?

At all events it must be observed that nearly fifty of Virginia Woolf's hundred years have passed without bringing forth a single native English female poet of any outstanding quality. The sexist critic would say that the woman writer is by her nature more prosaic, long-winded and tale-bearing, the male writer gifted with a superior verbal and constructional ability, so that the genius of one "naturally" expresses itself through story-telling, the other through poetry. Hardly; there are not so many male poets either, worthy the title in recent years. Historical and cultural factors determine the form and medium through which a genius finds its expression, and not merely sexual. It seems that ours is a prose age, at least in England, not unlike the way in which the eighteenth century was, for the novel as a form has a similar relevance to our needs now as it had in the era which developed it. The novel is, pre-eminently, the twentieth-century form, *the* contemporary mode for writers today; and most writers adopt it for this reason, whether they are male or female.

It is no more encouraging to consider the question of women dramatists, who are even more thin on the ground than women poets. Aphra Behn shines virtually alone and rather dimly down the dark centuries to the present day, remembered but never performed; and even the "emancipated" twentieth century can really boast only Enid Bagnold, Lillian Hellman, Ann Jellicoe, and Shelagh Delaney, all of whom should probably be seen as contemporary phenomena rather than as enduring artists. Why should this be so? Pehaps it is to be linked with the female lack of spatial or constructional ability as alleged by sexist psychologists. Male supremacists would doubtless interpret it as yet another expression of innate female inferiority, in that women simply cannot succeed in the "higher" form of drama, demanding as it does a total and continuous objectivity which women are so often assured that they find it difficult to achieve or maintain. The most likely explanation is that despite late twentieth-century pieties women are still far indeed from attaining that level of socio-cultural, educational, and economic freedom enjoyed by men. They are, too, still under pressure to conform to traditional concepts of womanly behaviour, to be self-effacing, supportive, and unjudging. Writing a novel is a far less assertive act than making a play, in that it does not need any further action or contribution to fulfil it. Novel writing is compatible with the conventional requirement of women that they should keep their heads down.

The almost complete absence of women humorists from the scene may support this hypothesis. Dorothy Parker is a bitter ironist rather than a comedy writer, and Caryl Brahms and Stella Gibbons similarly do not create comedy pure and complex as some male writers do. Could we imagine a female Wodehouse, for example, or a female Waugh? There is in addition the undeniable fact that a considerable amount of female literary talent has traditionally been channelled elsewhere than into "creative" writing. Women have for centuries been among the most prolific and successful of letter-writers and diarists, but it would seem, despite the cult success of Anais Nin, that these activities were and are not thought of as writing in the formal sense. We should also take into account the importance if not pre-eminence of women in the fields of children's stories and detective fiction. All this could be construed as a classic illustration of feminine underachieving—the creative drive finds its outlet in surreptitious, unacknowledged, or unimportant productions. There is, too, the basic physiological act of creation, which art has assumed as its own central metaphor;

many women, without any doubt, feel, like the mother of the Gracchi, that their children are their jewels and all the adornment that they need.

At the present stage of our knowledge of the springs of emotional and intellectual growth, of the processes of creativity and the origins of individualism, it is not possible to take these remarks beyond the stage of speculation and enquiry. Probably due to the emergence of the novel as a bourgeois form, coinciding with the emancipation of women as a bourgeois movement, the novel has engrossed the attention of the majority of women writers to the virtual exclusion of any other art form. This fact has been of substantial significance to all who work in this area. The sex of a novelist is always in question somewhere, sometime, in the course of the critical response. That this is not true of women poets and dramatists is attributable to the smallness of their numbers discussed above. Paradoxically, these isolated women have not, as might be expected, commanded attention because of their sex; their rarity has meant that they have been entirely overlooked as women. Criticism, in very recently an entirely male province, has dealt with creative women by treating them as males, and the exiguous band has been surrounded and absorbed without trace into the masculine act of making plays or poems.

But the history of the novel has been different from this. It has not been possible for criticism to ignore women novelists. Indeed, the sex of a novelist has for the last hundred years and more been so important as to join with considerations of a writer's epoch and social class to form the basis of any committed observation. We see a tension originating in the nineteenth century, when many women had to deny or disguise their female identity. The lady novelist picked up her pen as soon as her male colleague, but by the middle of the nineteenth century she had become the object of surprise, scorn, or roguish gallantry on all sides. Considerable interest was aroused by the hope of spotting a female hand at work, as Dickens did with George Eliot's *Scenes From Clerical Life* (1857). Masculine opinion combined to produce an impression of the woman writer as an aberration; the philistine gibe of W. S. Gilbert in *The Mikado* at the "lady novelist" as a "singular anomaly" who could well be spared from the cutural scene is not merely characteristic of the self-consciously low-brow tone adopted in deference to the operetta audience's known limitations of taste. The same note was sounded by Max Beerbohm as he gathered in the whole range of female ability with his sweeping assessment of Ouida: "Ouida is essentially feminine, as much *une femme des femmes* as Jane Austen or 'John Oliver Hobbes', and it is indeed remarkable that she should yet be endowed with force and energy so exuberant and indefatigable" (*English Critical Essays, Twentieth Century*, ed. Phyllis M. Jones, 1933, p. 179).

This sense of the strangeness of women writers persists even today, a suspicious unease alternating with a delighted admiration. Remarks like Jimmy Porter's description of a male acquaintance as "like a female Emily Brontë", or Irving Wardle's reference to *Gone With The Wind* as "a remarkable performance for a woman" demonstrate our casual acceptance of it. Recently, too, Beerbohm's antique surprise was echoed by Anthony Burgess: "It is rarely that one finds such a variety of gifts in one contemporary woman writer—humour, poetry, the power of the exact image, the ability to be both hard and compassionate, a sense of place, all the tricks of impersonation and, finally, a historical eye" (*The Novel Now*, 1967, p. 95). It would seem that the possession of all these gifts has been rare in any writer since Shakespeare went back to Stratford, but that does not decrease Burgess's surprise at finding a *woman* of such capacity.

Many would concede that the sense of sex difference was strong in the past, but feel that on the whole, things are different now. The idea of the "lady novelist", like the phrase itself, has a whiff of stale elegance and misplaced chivalry about it. The days are gone in which a male critic could no more bring himself to dispraise a lady's novel than he could express dislike of her bonnet. Those familiar with Norman Mailer's critique of Mary McCarthy in *Cannibals and Christians* (1967), pp. 133–40, and his general response to his female critics in *The Prisoner Of Sex* (1971), will be aware that they are gone indeed; Mailer can bring himself to the entire critical gamut that lies between the left hook and the right cross.

Times change. So do habits of style. Distinction between writers on grounds of sex has now become *démodé* as an overt act of critical observation. Facile distinctions in this area are frowned

41

upon as much by psychology as by literary criticism. The crudity and obviousness of using the differentiation of artists on grounds of sex as a starting point well fits this critical device for the world of journalism where it now does its most apparent work—who is not familiar with the admiring interview of a well-known woman writer, conducted with an arch tone of surprise and much explication of how she does it? (See, for example, the article on Elizabeth Jane Howard, "All Her Own Work", *The Times*, Monday, March 20th 1972.) Sex definition as a major theme of the twentieth-century novel has reinforced consciousness of women writers, as has the increasingly explicit treatment of sex itself; the hotter the beans, the more interest in who is spilling them.

Then, too, we must reckon with something that still holds true for most, despite some spectacular individual escapes, the continued social subjugation of women. The persistence of the historical refusal to grant them much significant agency either alone or as a group, has helped to ensure that the part-playful, part-hostile nineteenth-century distinction of "lady novelist", with all the attendant condescending discussion of female "spheres of influence" and so on, has stayed very much alive. But it seems to have made its way from the forefront of the mind into the vaster swell of sub-rational apprehension where it can do infinitely more harm. Better to have the separatist concept lodged visibly in the middle of the intellectual backwoodsman's armoury, than to have it operating subliminally on the judgments of the don, who claims not to think in these terms, but who always knows others who do.

It is of course incontrovertible that there is an order of genius in which the sex of the possessor is irrelevant. It is equally true that most writers do not get anywhere near it. The supreme talent rebukes the reader and compels silence; the lesser has to compete for our attention with the resources that are to hand. This is not to say that we never think of Emily Brontë as a woman, or Tolstoy as a man, but that the books themselves do not continuously remind us that we are reading the product of female or male. With minor writers we tend to notice more the intrusion of the author as a presence, sexual or otherwise; and certain novels depend substantially for their effect upon the *frisson* pro-

42

duced by our awareness of the author's sex in tension or contrast with his material: consider *The Group* (1963), where the female author's consistent belittling of the female sex results in an alternation of the writer's stance between the (masculine?) mode of detached and authoritative assessment ("the inside voice of one who knows"), and the arguably feminine mode of closely engaged comment, almost of personal malice ("yes, it's true that women are all bitches").

Consciousness of sex difference is as marked as ever it was. For sex difference itself shows no sign of abandoning its position in the centre of cultural awareness—how could it? Do we think then of male and female writers? No: The distinction has become hallowed as "writers" and "women writers". This, the twentieth-century descendant of the "lady novelist" phrasing and approach of the nineteenth century, has continued to confine creative women to a pejorative subsection of literature long after they were, technically at least, admitted to certain social and legal equalities. It may be neither possible nor desirable to work towards some kind of critical or creative fusion of the sexes so that we become less aware of the sex of a writer in our response to the work. But we should at least wake up to some of the different ways in which we assess on sex grounds. Sex-based critical processes are of particular importance to women writers, since they are usually disadvantaged by these hidden assumptions and unacknowledged criteria. The process is deftly exposed by Ivy Compton-Burnett in *Men And Wives* (1931); the initiated will observe a characteristic Compton-Burnett joke in the deliberate use of the author with whom she has herself most frequently been linked:

"What do you think of Miss Jane Austen's books, Jermyn?" said Dominic—"if I may approach so great a man upon a comparatively flimsy subject."

"Our row of green books with the pattern on the backs, Rachel?" said Sir Percy with a sense of adequacy in conversation. "Very old-fashioned, aren't they?"

"What do the ladies think of the author, the authoress, for she is of their own sex?" said Dominic.

"I have a higher standard for greatness," said Agatha, "but I don't deny she has great qualities. I give her the word great in that sense."

43

'You put that very well, Mrs Calkin," said Dominic. "I feel I must become acquainted with the fair writer."

"That is a great honour for her!" said Geraldine.

(p. 94)

Note that the reader of this is not only made aware of the writer's sex in the abstract—Jane Austen was a "lady novelist" —but is also shown how it conditions each individual's response in terms of his or her own sex. As Dominic illustrates, a certain type of man approaches a woman's novel as if it were a woman, flirtatiously, but not forgetting the demands of chivalry. Mary Ellman has detected a similar process in criticism, when, in dealing with a woman writer, it "embarks, at its happiest, upon an intellectual measuring of busts and hips" (p. 29). Ivy Compton-Burnett throughout her work nudges her readers into the realisation of the part their own sex plays in their response to a writer, in the establishing of the dialogue of any fiction between creator and recipient; although true to her sybilline persona she never called herself anything more flamboyantly sexual than "I. Compton-Burnett".

Sex difference is of course only part of the basic equipment which each writer brings to the task of being a novelist. It may not be a major conditioning influence; social class, with all its contingent effects upon education, leisure, self-esteem, and life expectations, is clearly an enormous thing to come to terms with, and in all its potential refinements likely to affect as many facets of the novelist's production as merely being male or female does. Even in what we think of as the more rigidly structured society of the nineteenth century, Parson Austen's daughter led a very different life from Parson Brontë's, only a few years earlier. It is the distinctive setting of the life that will shape the fiction —Charlotte's from its first years so full of the standard horrors of Victorian everyday life, and of unbearable blows so continuously borne, Jane's existence so apparently undisturbed.

This last, though, like Ivy Compton-Burnett's claim to have led a life so uneventful that there was nothing to put in a biography, must be deceptive; Elizabeth Sprigge's authorised version, *The Life of Ivy Compton-Burnett* (1973), clearly shows up the nature of this deception but is all too reticent, alas, to indicate its extent. All lives are eventful, unless we fall into the vulgar fallacy of excluding all but terminal or sensational acts from view. Drama and significance are extrinsic qualities which Jane Austen understood as well as any other writer how to produce; see the memorable and justly famous moment at the end of Chapter XVIII of *Mansfield Park*, when the illicit thespians are electrified by these simple monosyllables: "My father is come! He is in the hall at this moment." Sir Thomas is here fully embodied in the minds of all and not only in Fanny's fearful apprehension, as the threatening masculine principle of vengeance and punishment. It is the measure of his moral progress in the novel that he is permitted to shake off his association with the novel's other egotistic and destructive males, and develop an adherence to that area of the emotional action in which Edmund links with Fanny in his passive and superficially unimpressive virtue, as well as in his capacity for standing by an "undesirable" decision; and Mary Crawford, Edmund's personal *lamia*, has as much power to disturb and distort his life as her brother has over Fanny. All the key moments in Jane Austen readily lend themselves to analysis in terms of a variety of significances; it seems likely that the full sexual implications of her writing have not yet been uncovered.

Nevertheless a parson's daughter will obviously lead a different life from a parson's son, and sex difference has been vital, though usually in unperceived ways, in conditioning attitudes, both of the writer towards his characters and themes, and of the readers towards the writer. There seems to be an inescapable ambivalence or confusion in our thinking on this subject. The sex of a writer may be something we never consider, but it is also something we never forget. We may not think of "George Eliot" as a lady novelist (though possibly the subliminal effects of the masculine name should not be underestimated; such pressures seem to be at work in the case of Stevie Smith whose deliberately intersex name leads many of those who do not know to think her male). But do we think of Jane Austen in this way? Virginia Woolf?

The great artists may illustrate the absurdity and pettiness of such classification, but they will be able to do little to undermine it. It is the more ironic that there has never been any basis shown for establishing or continuing such a division. Various studies have appeared which could be expected to tackle the question of whether or not there is such a thing as a distinctively feminine

45

style. Marjory Bald's *Women-Writers of the Nineteenth Century* (1923), Muriel Masefield's *Women Novelists from Fanny Burney to George Eliot* (1934), and more recently Vineta Colby's *The Singular Anomaly* (1970), are among books which have considered women writers in a group, as if their sex must have some significance, or provide some common factor to their work, and then make no attempt to discover what it is. The usual form is to announce their intention to treat their subjects not as sexual beings, but as "authors only", and the illogic of a procedure which undermines their central premise of selection goes unnoticed.

They may have been deterred, however, by contemplating the difficulties of those who have tried. The critics who have made the attempt upon this north face of commentary predictably find themselves perpetuating existing concepts of contemporary behaviour rather than illuminating the secrets of mental activity:

> The new woman, the feminine novelist of the twentieth century, has abandoned the old realism. She does not accept *observed* revelation. She is seeking, with passionate determination, for that Reality which is behind the material, the things that matter, spiritual things, ultimate Truth. And here she finds man an outsider, wilfully blind, purposely indifferent. Not that her own conceptions, or definitions, are yet by any means definite or clearly formulated. Speaking generally, I think one may say that she is striving to see and express, all that part of life and humanity which formal Religion once claimed to interpret.
>
> (R. Brimley Johnson, *Some Contemporary Novelists, Women*, 1920, pp. xiv–xv)

The new woman, on closer inspection, proves to be our old friend, the Angel at the Hearth. How difficult it is for all women except witches and whores to shake off this time-honoured female role of custodian of the moral values, sensitive to "the things that matter"! Social notions of appropriate role behaviour vitiate this as a critical attempt to discern thematic preoccupations.

One of the few critics to make a genuine effort to isolate and describe the specifically female qualities of women's writing was W. L. Courtney. His comments in *The Feminine Note In Fiction* (1904) amply illustrate his inherited prejudices. He asserts that there does exist " a distinctively feminine style in fiction", "of a type peculiarly its own". This style is inferior to that achieved by male novelists, since the female writer cannot transcend the limits of the immediate: "the beginning of a woman's work is generally the writing of a personal diary"—"would it be wrong to say that a woman's heroine is always a glorified version of herself?" She is further restricted by the narrowness of her perception and understanding; "a passion for detail is the distinguishing mark of nearly every female novelist" (little things please little minds, perhaps). Women's novels are deficient in construction, since their authors cannot take the broad view; the female intellect cannot strain so far; "it is the neutrality of the artistic mind which the female novelist seems to find it so difficult to realise". Naturally, difficulties of tone result: "the female author is at once self-conscious and didactic". Women writers should stick to their little squares of ivory; Courtney sees the female genius as expressed best in the "novels of manners" like Jane Austen's. Women can be equal or indeed superior at "miniature-work", but inferior on the "large canvas". Women should also recognise that their essential nobility is best shown not in writing but in their readiness to subordinate and sacrifice themselves to duty.

Courtney's uninformed condescension and failure of objectivity can most charitably be seen as the unquestioned and undigested assumptions of his time. Anthony Burgess has no such historical figleaf with which to cover his naked attitudes. In his study *The Novel Now* (1967), Burgess restricts the entire range of women novelists to one chapter, coyly entitled "Yin and Yang". Note the Lawrentian flavour of his summary of the "big contemporary theme" of women writers:

> Woman has a sexual need of man, but she objects to having this need; she wants to reject man, but she cannot, and so she seeks to dominate him, though a good great deal of her sexual fulfilment must derive from being dominated. *Yin* and *Yang* are tangled up together, and the literary expression of the female dilemma is often harsh, sensational, explosive.
>
> (p. 122)

It is difficult to conceive of a pronouncement upon women writers which could contrive so well to be unfair simultaneously to Pamela Hansford Johnson and to Brigid Brophy, to Elizabeth Bowen and to Doris Lessing. But this is not meant to be unflattering. "Harsh, sensational, explosive", are all terms of praise in Burgess's critical vocabulary; all good qualities are masculine and all masculine qualities good. Hence "guts" is both a term of high approbation and the chief indication that a masculine controlling intelligence (?) is at work (women for the purposes of this metaphor being understood as devoid of the standard viscera). Burgess's stereotyped notions of women writers are further revealed by his conclusion:

> We have tended to regard clarity and common sense as essentially feminine proporties in the novel—Alice in a land of male jabberwocks. Some of our traditionalists among women . . . have made our sweating male experimentalists look gauche and uncomfortable. But, if the art of the novel is to progress, there will have to be sweat and discomfort. The *Yin* cannot have all its own way.
>
> (pp. 129–30)

This passage contains a series of belittling assumptions—women writers are all Jane Austens if not Alices in Wonderland—and it is informed throughout by that primitive sense of superiority which is not assailable by rational processes. By some extension of what is usually admiringly referred to as masculine logic, a sweating struggling male novelist is not only the owner of this land in which the women wander, Alice-like; his effort alone represents the future of the novel, in his "sweat and discomfort" lies the creative effort (see again how these physical manifestations are not only abrogated to the male, as if women never sweat or struggle, but are also held up as criteria of excellence, demonstrations of potency and the capacity to become deeply involved in the struggle for mastery over the brute inertia of the raw material— sexual analogy again). But the defensive note in the last line clearly points up the embattled nature of Burgess's thinking. The novel is felt to be masculine territory which the man must keep control of (cf. Mailer's "Great Bitch"). The *"yin"* must not call the tune. Nor must females break out of their traditional compounds. Doris Lessing, one of the few women writers whose style has been generally considered as approximating, through its aggression, drive, and scope, rather to a "masculine" than a "feminine" mode, is handled with a mixture of the reproachful, the sarcastic, and the dismissive. Writing of Anna, the heroine of *The Golden Notebook*, he says:

> Her conception of herself as a "free woman" leads her to say some hard things about male arrogance, crassness, sexual impotence and incompetence, and her own sexual frustrations (which are, of course, to be blamed on men) fill up a good part of one notebook. She is intelligent, honest, burning with conviction, but she ends up as a bit of a bore. So for that matter, does Mrs Lessing's own experiment.

(p. 100)

Who will be surprised to learn that among Burgess's other pet aversions top of the list comes Brigid Brophy?

Burgess is an extreme case, but he is not alone in his attitudes. Many critics feel vaguely that there is something odd or threatening about women writers; "Who's afraid of Virginia Woolf?" is apparently a key question of our time. Edward Albee's anti-feminism is treated fully by Katharine Rogers in her study of misogyny in literature, *The Troublesome Helpmate* (1966); what is interesting here is that he found Virginia Woolf a particularly appropriate peg to hang his preoccupations on. It shows, too, that hostility towards intelligent females is not simply the idiosyncrasy of the old fogey still fostering ancient grudges against suffragettes and bluestockings. It seems to be rediscovered by every generation of creative men, and is perhaps rather to be seen as a logical extension of the assumption that literary creation is itself a masculine act, a process of exploring and mastering the feminine, unconscious mass of life and material. Hence any woman who tries this and succeeds in it contradicts the unacknowledged laws of kind—it should not be in the nature of the beast to behave so. Lord David Cecil has remarked in conversation how frequently people comment unfavourably upon Jane Austen's unmarried state and childlessness, taking it to be a failure of full humanity that she did not assume these dimensions. It is felt to be unfortunate that she did not marry, while we should more reasonably consider it unfortunate, on the basis of their matrimonial records, that Dickens, Hardy, or Tolstoy did.

Criticism seems to have to come to terms with women writers in every new age, and is pleased to treat each fresh generation of women writers as if they were the first of their sex to pick up the pen. It is not the least interesting aspect of women's writing that its very existence has continually to be explained (away?). Both critical and authorial comment repeatedly raises and tries to answer the question, "Why do women write novels?" The conventional answer, as we have seen, is that the rise of the novel was roughly contemporaneous with the emancipation of women; motive and opportunity coincided. Hazel Mews, in *Frail Vessels* (1969), draws attention to the fact that women novelists first appeared in any numbers or quality during the years of revolutionary upheaval at the beginning of the nineteenth century (Mary Wollstonecraft's *Vindication of the Rights of Woman* had appeared in 1792). Mews comments cautiously:

> It seems at least probable that the upheaval in old ways of thought in the minds of women should provide some release of power for works of the imagination, the response of the women writers matching the dynamic of the transitional changes that confronted them.
>
> (pp. 5–6)

Ivy Compton-Burnett has already similarly linked the development of women's writing in the twentieth century with the devastating cataclysm that marked its opening years. Speaking of becoming established as a novelist in the period after the First World War, she attributed women's success starkly to a far more horrific social convulsion than female emancipation:

> . . . the men were dead, you see, and the women didn't marry so much because there was no one for them to marry, and so they had leisure, and, I think in a good many cases they had money, because their brothers were dead, and all that would tend to writing, wouldn't it, being single, and having some money, and having the time—having no men, you see.
>
> (Kay Dick, *Ivy and Stevie*, 1971, p. 7)

This seems to imply that she felt that women of her time owed most of their prominence to the massive male mortality without which they would have been overwhelmed by the men in one way or another. Or perhaps the suggestion is rather that women need some external event of great reverberance to awake them from their long sleep of history to the fullness of their potential—Eve's dream of truth?

Certainly the nineteenth century first saw women turning to the writing of novels as a job. Aphra Behn is often held up as the first female professional writer in that she (largely) supported herself by her writing, but it is not until the nineteenth century that women writers existed in any numbers as professionals, and even as hacks. Again and again we hear of women resorting to writing to support their families, and novel-production becomes indeed a genteel cottage industry in the central decades of this century; Mrs Frances Trollope, mother of Anthony, turned out one hundred and fifteen volumes of fiction, commentary, and poetry, and she by no means holds the record. Dorothy Parker cast a typically beady gaze upon this tradition of the phenomenally competent and productive woman writer in A Pig's-Eye View of Literature:

> The pure and worthy Mrs Stowe,
> Is one we all are proud to know
> As mother, wife, and authoress—
> Thank God, I am content with less!

Harriet Beecher Stowe is assured of her small corner in literary history, but most of these amazingly industrious and copious women have not held their own with time as their more gifted sisters have. Who now recalls Lucas Malet, Gertrude Atherton, Voynich, or Miss Mary Wilkins, in comparison with George Eliot?—but they are, in almost all respects, far more typical of their period than she was.

Does this mean, then, because women were writing novels in such vast numbers, and in that sense keeping up with male writers, that there was then established a feminine tradition in novel writing? Raymond Williams has stated his belief that in the nineteenth century the work of women writers was invaluable in keeping alive and reaffirming the needs and terms not simply of a woman's world, but in certain vital ways a human world. But again, this is simply a picture of what is itself a Victorian stereotype of womanhood, the lady with the lamp, the guardian of true values, ceaselessly and unobtrusively about her task of disseminating sweetness and light. Williams himself agrees that the achieved mode of society was a masculine one, and any female productions had necessarily to conform to the externally imposed requirements not only of a masculine society at large, but more immediately to the terms of male publishers, critics, and editors. It is often asserted that as women were excluded from the social and political functioning of the dominant and shaping masculine world, so they expressed themselves creatively through the novel. This is true up to a point, but the point is a vital one; they were not allowed to expressed themselves *as women*.

Again, such truth as there is in Williams's statement applies only to the really great women writers of the time. Most of us would agree that *Middlemarch* expresses, particularly towards its close, an ascending series of moments which are little short of sublime; and George Eliot consistently displays in her writing a fullness of humanity if any writer does. But she herself never committed the narrow sectarian fault of attributing this to her femininity, or saw herself as founding or contributing to a specifically female tradition of writing. There was no attempt to avoid the oppressive contemporary difficulties of women—"A woman must choose meaner things, because only meaner things are offered to her"— and at times her characters speak of the humiliations of women with a bitterness which it is tempting to regard as personal:

> You are not a woman. You may try—but you can never imagine what it is to have a man's force of genius in you, and yet to suffer the slavery of being a girl. To have a pattern cut out—". . . this is what you must be; this is what you are wanted for; a woman's heart must be of such a size and no larger, else it must be pressed small, like Chinese feet; her happiness is to be made as cakes are, by a fixed receipt".
>
> (*Daniel Deronda*, Book VII, Chapter I)

But this was only one of any number of themes as far as George Eliot was concerned, and she always sought to be free of any close involvement with the feminist movement of her time, either in life or in literature. Thus, while she contributed substantially to the foundation of Girton College, she remained tepid about female suffrage, and although her work must surely escape any classification as "woman's writing", she was sensitive about and strict towards "Silly Novels by Lady Novelists", in the title of her famous essay. At no point in her work does George Eliot ever address her reader in anything that sounds like a woman's voice. What she strives for, and perfectly accomplishes, is the "masculine" mode, that of the detached, educated, omniscient outsider. She writes as an honorary male, largely assuming the values and processes of the male-created and dominated society of her time. Her sympathy for women and keen sense of their wrongs is an important element in her writing; but it is hardly more than might have been expressed by any thoughtful man of her age, or earlier.

It is easier to make out a case for Charlotte Brontë as the founding or Great Earth Mother of a feminine tradition in the nineteenth century. Ironically, it is she and not George Eliot who strenuously asserted the principle of authorial anonymity and independence: "To you I am neither man nor woman—I come before you as author only. It is the sole standard by which you have a right to judge me—the sole ground on which I accept your judgment" (*The Brontës, Their Lives, Friendships and Correspondence*, edited by T. J. Wise and J. A. Symington, Oxford, 1932, III, 11). But the taut rhythms and defensive stance of this plainly show that Charlotte knew, for herself if not for all women, that the impersonal equals the impossible. Charlotte's work has lent itself to feminist exegesis first because of the centrality of females in her thought. All her novels can crudely be summed up as dealing with a woman in search of her identity. This search is interpreted more widely and fluently than had previously seemed possible for heroines of English fiction; independence, its definition and accomplishment (still a major feminist theme today), is worked through with an obsessive passion which can still startle and persuade. There is a perennial relevance in her heroines' attempts to define their identity, and in the stress, particularly through Lucy Snowe, on the importance of work in establishing even a tenuous self-esteem. In *Shirley* (1849), her picture of Emily, we have a novel which, as Hazel Mews puts it, "can almost be regarded as an artificially contrived vehicle for the expression of Charlotte Brontë's views on the intellectual and emotional privations of women".

It is also through her female characters that Charlotte outlines her ideas of the entire operation of loving, feeling, suffering, and aspiring. Her men may clench their fists, furrow their brows, and even, *in extremis*, send love-calls through time and space

53

to the beloved woman, as Rochester does. But all this is externally observed, and at times strikes us as contrived. Charlotte's deepest and most authoritative communication of genuine human feeling is invariably expressed through women; in her fiction, only the women have full souls.

But it is not simply that Charlotte deals in a detailed and convincing way with feminist themes, nor that she chooses women to bear her main thematic burdens. Much of the tension of her fiction, as of her sisters', arises from the clash between her heroines' compulsion towards self-fulfilment and their neurotic attraction towards masochism and self-sacrifice. The impulse to struggle is matched evenly with the urge to submit. As *Jane Eyre* is her best known story, it may seem that the message to resist the St John Rivers of this world would have come through loud and clear to women readers. But his is only one form of masculine dominance, a bloodless negation of the sexual principle which Jane, despite the airy symbolic associations of her surname, cannot bear to have forced upon her. Is it in any sense an option for the ideal of female freedom that Charlotte at the end of the novel consigns her heroine to the arms of the dark and dominant Rochester, maimed and tamed, it is true, but still recognisably the same thrilling brute who stalks so potently through the fiction and fantasy of all the Brontë sisters?

Perhaps Jane's freedom is no more than this, the right to choose who is to dominate her. In any case, her union with Rochester, not to mention the obligatory appearance of the beautiful offspring, while satisfactory in terms of the conventions of the fiction, cannot help but produce the residual disappointment which we also experience at the end of *Middlemarch*, constrained as we are to ask, is this all? Is all the struggle and suffering, all the intense effort and loss of peace, merely to be seen as apprenticeship to marriage? Was it really the most that nineteenth-century women could hope for, the right to gain the man whom they could love and live with? Certainly there are occasions in her fiction when Charlotte is prepared to offer not only marriage but doglike submission as the apotheosis of her heroine's emotional career; consider the climax of *Shirley*, where Louis, again rather like Will Ladislaw in *Middlemarch*, is sufficiently enthused by the strength of a rich woman's love for him to bring himself to overlook "gold and her station":

"My pupil," I said.
"My master," was the low answer.

(Chapter 36)

Low indeed. Nor are things improved by subsequent references to the man as the woman's "keeper". This fairly constant hinting at the need to submit as a main aspect of female nature, together with odd glimpses of hysteria, morbid excess of feeling, and masochism, have also strengthened Charlotte's claim to be among the first writers in a feminine, if not feminist, tradition. It is interesting in this context that this element of Charlotte's work is still relevant and suggestive today. Jean Rhys, herself noted for her preference for neo-masochistic and damaged heroines, the walking wounded of the sex war, has written the story of Rochester's first wife in *Wide Sargasso Sea* (1966). This novel reworks and even reconditions the relationship between the two in a way which comments ironically on Charlotte's emphasis of treatment. Charlotte uses mad Bertha not only as a main element and eventually the explanation of the Gothic mystery and horror of the story; her other principal function is to obtain sympathy for Rochester, and to reinforce the picture of him as a man betrayed and abused by women—Bertha's mental decay is linked with the faithlessness of Céline Varens and the self-seeking of Blanche Ingram as examples of what Jane restores and cleanses him from. Charlotte focuses on the man, and like the other former loves of Rochester, Bertha is a flat character, almost diagrammatically drawn.

Jean Rhys reverses this. She gives us a Bertha (rehabilitated under the more attractive, less damning name of Antoinette) who has been a lifelong victim of a male-dominated society. Jean Rhys reminds us, as Charlotte does not, that a blasted and hopeless marriage happens to two people. This haunting and painful story, charting as it does Antoinette's involvement, suffering, and despair, is not simply the story that Charlotte chose not to write; it is one she could not have written, and perfectly illustrates her inability to achieve a genuinely feminist standpoint. For her writing, like her society, is fundamentally male-oriented. Even her

55

heroines' much-vaunted freedom is defined on masculine terms; her successful women are always those who can take on the "man's world" according to its own rules, and survive. They fight with masculine weapons of courage and self-assertion for masculine rights of liberty and work. Nowhere in Charlotte's fiction is there any attempt to challenge these assumptions of her society in ways which insist on appropriately *feminine* modes of self-expression. It is significant that when, in *Villette*, she nerved herself to bring about a sad ending, she bowed ultimately to her father's intervention in favour of the more conventional conclusion.

I am not here attacking Charlotte for not being what she never wanted or tried to be. It is the view that she writes "as a woman" that is under fire. Nor does she only support the conventional assumptions in her use of the traditional theme of the woman's need of man. More important, perhaps, is her management of the romance form as a vehicle for her ideas. This is not a reference to her use of Gothic detail in her tales, but to her consistent effort to create that remote and strange world which appeals to its readers on the less than conscious level, dealing with deeply-felt needs and urges, and at its highest attaining almost the status of myth. In Charlotte's fiction there are no literal monsters, maidens in chains, and chests of gold and jewels. But the experience of love is the voyage through the foreign land where the stranger wanders lost and afraid. Other people, the unpredictable convolutions of their personalities and the hidden and often threatening secrets of their psyches, constitute the demon-haunted caverns, the pagan temples, and the dragon-infested forests. Romance conventions too dictate her characters' fondness for what might unsympathetically be interpreted as posturing, and her weakness (or, more probably, strength) for extremes of language and situation. It is the romance element in Charlotte's work which either enslaves or alienates her reader; either we thrill to her claim, made through her characters' presented belief in self-discovery as the major creative act of the individual, that she is giving us "not 'a story' but the truth", in Karl Kroeber's phrase; or else we are inclined to resist what strikes us as overstated and even a little absurd. It indicates precisely the nature and extent of Charlotte's gift that she was able to work in the romance tradition with such subtlety and abandon; but her potency derives from her recapturing the old rather than building the new. So far from directing the novel into the uncharted waters of the feminist revolution, Charlotte was the writer who accomplished its decisive and significant link with the oldest and most magical of fictional forms.

Charlotte's achievement in bringing the modern novel into romance, or romance into the novel, did have one effect of peculiar importance for the development of women's writing as a whole. It assisted the division of women's writing into two genres, the "honorary male" mode, as exemplified by George Eliot, in which the writer largely assumes the standards and values of the masculine society, and the "feminine" mode dealing with romance themes in a muted romance form, which concentrates on, and comes to define, woman's "proper sphere". Romance, traditionally, depends upon involving the reader in a subjective experience. It offers imaginative release at the price of objectivity and detachment; but as it usually features centrally an *ideal* of behaviour, it deals in instruction as well as escapism. Its happy ending is a conscious artistic attempt to make a stand against the misery and messiness of realism by the brief satisfaction of desires and hopes which cannot be accommodated within the real life of organised society. In earlier romance (Spenser, Sidney, Shakespeare) both men and women alike experience these fairy lands and their demands and dangers. Charlotte's almost exclusive concentration on women led imperceptibly to a situation in which romance becomes *the* female form, the form chosen for fiction written by, for, and about women.

This process is further reflected in the degeneration of the word "romance" itself. Once evocative of all that was wonderful and strange, it now signifies in modern usage a story whose stress is upon love and a female's emotional development, with marriage as the ultimate destiny and solution. In defiance of its parent form, modern "true love romance" tends to play down and to exclude disturbing material, concentrating on the exaltation of the familiar and the enhancing of the ordinary. A. S. Byatt, in *Degrees of Freedom* (1965), has said that the function of this type of romance, as peddled in women's magazines and cheap paperbacks, is "to console"; it seems plain that it is also intended

57

to define, to delimit and prohibit. The young girl is constantly urged to settle for the plain boy next door; the wife is warned against the dangers of getting dissatisfied with her dull and worthy husband. At the same time the appetite for the remote and the exciting is satisfied with material concentrating upon foreign holidays, the past (Regency times seem especially suited to glamorous treatment), or even simply "life in London"; all these are presumed to seem indiscriminately marvellous to the housewife or office junior in Stoke-on-Trent.

It is easy to deride this type of fiction, and any reader, male or female, who has any pretensions to critical standards soon learns to develop a reflex disdain for anything which can be described as "woman's magazine stuff". What seems less obvious, however, is the extent to which a great deal of serious fiction is in fact the same stuff writ large (or small). This type of modern "romance" is by no means confined to *Woman* and *Woman's Own*. It forms the staple of the work of such respectable figures as Enid Bagnold and Pamela Hansford Johnson, and is at least intermittently present in the efforts of Susan Hill, and even Iris Murdoch. It is also the convention which has to be understood as the basis for nearly all of Muriel Spark's fiction; she assumes our familiarity with its precepts in order to be able to undercut and diminish them. Modern romance is as this suggests very much the province of women writers. The particular blend of yearning, suffering, compromising, and self-comforting is very much related to the quality of female lives, both of readers and writers. As a consequence, by the social rule that dictates that as soon as an activity becomes largely a female one, men will increasingly cease to practise it, male writers have on the whole abandoned romance (except at the lowliest Mills and Boon level).

This interesting historical development, with its important related side-effects both for women and men writers, was largely accomplished in the nineteenth century as a result of the fiction of Charlotte Brontë. Hers was not the only formative influence, nor was it purely the problem of her lifetime. Jane Austen was conscious of having inherited a tradition whose limits and limitations she accepted only up to a certain point. Hers may seem to be the archetypal "romance fiction". The truth universally acknowledged that a single man in possession of a good fortune must be

58

in want of a wife, depends on an awareness of all the single girls in want of a husband. Marriage in all its variations is the cornerstone of her moral and imaginative structures, so much so that it may seem that she accepts quite uncritically the social prescriptions of her time. This impression is reinforced by a consideration of the extent to which Jane Austen internalised and even elevated the fiscal obsessions of her contemporaries. In his essay "Fiction and the Analogical Matrix", in *The World We Imagine* (1969), Mark Schorer has shown through detailed evaluation that Jane Austen's novels all have "a stylistic base derived from commerce and property, the counting house and the inherited estate". This metaphorical substructure is so pervasive that we find even the most dead of metaphors or most colourless of figures of speech being vitalised to contribute to the overall effect. Significantly, too, "moral qualities are persistently put in economic figures".

But a subtler reading of Jane's fiction shows how consistently she queries and even reverses the agreed social assumptions. She never makes her good characters break conventions with a genuine moral basis, but has no patience with the Bingleys' feeling that Lizzy should not walk alone through muddy fields to her sick sister's bedside. Through Mrs Elton, with her lamentable absence of "elegance of mind", she shows how the pursuit of conventional delicacy can itself become a coarse vulgarism. She endorses, too, through her main characters, marriages which are not really so conventional and respectable. Elizabeth and D'Arcy in *Pride and Prejudice* are not a good *social* match, and D'Arcy could have done much "better" in conventional terms; Jane Austen's picture of the De Bourghs shows her view of this "better" marriage and stresses the importance of ignoring extrinsic considerations.

The same is true of Emma and Knightley, Fanny and Edmund. The orthodox "romance" pairings are carefully drawn in for us— Emma and Frank Churchill, Edmund and Mary, Fanny and Henry —in order precisely to illustrate their inadequacy and to invite us to reject them as possibilities. Many times in her work Jane Austen leads us to disvalue or to reject the romance theme or motif in favour of the moral and human dimension. It is only as Emma awakens from her Sleeping Beauty trance that we get to know and like her as a human being. Her diminution in the social

59

scale of the novel—coming to tolerate the Coles family, and realising her actual inferiority to Miss Bates—is matched by her growing in the moral one. At the conclusion the received impression is surely intended to be that the village has lost a princess, but Knightley has gained a person.

Nor does the handsome prince do any better in Jane Austen's hands. The power of this deceptive old ideograph is conveyed through the brilliance of Wickham's initial impact on Lizzy and on women in general, and men too. Jane Austen has not succeeded in her aim unless the reader is likewise taken with him, for we are intended to share with Lizzy in her disillusion as the charm wears thin and the glitter drops away and she realises that she is in fact dealing with a toad, after all. Benwick in *Persuasion* is not so sternly handled—he has not offended like Wickham—but his stance as the ideal faithful lover of poetry and romance is never taken seriously, but gently tolerated as a phase he will come through, as indeed he does. *Persuasion* is Jane Austen's most interesting work in this context; this novel most strongly and feelingly asserts the supremacy of individual need over social and conventional requirements. On this occasion the "right" marriage, and how wrong it would have been, are fully shown in the younger Musgraves' ménage, and the theme is re-echoed in the treatment of Frank Elliot's worthlessness, as well as in the demonstration, through Wentworth's success, of how right the "wrong" marriage could have been. In treating the reawakening of an affection which if only slumbering in Anne's heart is quite cold in Wentworth's, Jane Austen set herself her most difficult task; but this theme also enabled her to make some of her sharpest and most derogatory comments on the hollowness of rank and position.

That Jane Austen was herself aware of the discrepancy between what was expected and what she produced is clear from one of her rare surviving observations upon the practice of fiction, in which she mocked the current if occasionally covert notion that even if women do not write in a certain way, they definitely ought to. Here is her "Plan of a novel according to hints from various quarters":

> Early in her career, the heroine must meet with the hero: all perfection, of course, and only prevented from paying his addresses

to her by some excess of refinement. Wherever she goes somebody falls in love with her, and she receives repeated offers of marriage, which she refers wholly to her father, exceedingly angry that *he* should not be the first applied to. Often carried away by the anti-hero, but rescued either by her father or the hero. Often reduced to support herself and her father by her talents, and work for her bread; continually cheated, and defrauded of her hire; worn down to a skeleton, and now and then starved to death.

(James Austen-Leigh, *Memoir of Jane Austen*, 1870, p. 164)

This is clearly the archetypal "woman's novel", the characteristic social details of the period notwithstanding. The assumption that the heroine's entire significance, not to mention future life, must be centred upon a man, is paramount. Equally axiomatic is the heroine's irresistibility. This summary also hints at the sado-masochistic element quietly present in most fiction of this type; the heroine has to suffer, to be at the mercy of a ruthless male, in order to stimulate and satisfy that somewhat unhealthy area of sexual fantasy, both male and female, which needs inequality as its pivot. The "woman's novel", by, for, and about a woman, is defined here with such wit and point that we can only regret that Jane Austen never wrote it.

Women writers have always been under the pressure of masculine society, even when they were as much loved and admired as Jane was. But it is in Charlotte's fiction that we see these pressures at work most clearly. Certainly she felt as a woman— there is a plaintive adolescent fantasy in the way in which her plain awkward heroines are at last rewarded with the "best" men —but she shaped her fictions as a man of her time would have done. She crystallises contemporary preoccupations about the "woman question" and in so doing automatically reflects the residual misogyny or at least distrust of certain types of woman which was widespread in her time. This feeling is even more evident among the very numerous less talented women writers of the nineteenth century. These tend to endorse the values of their male-dominated society strenuously, even at times hysterically. Most Victorian women writers, for instance, punish aberrant females quite sadistically; there was a savage hostility to emancipated women, the "girl of the period", in Mrs Eliza Lynn Linton's phrase. Mrs Humphry Ward's heroine in *The Marriage of William*

Ashe (1905) is a late example of a recurrent figure, the girl who through smoking, flirting, and leaving her husband for another man, brings on herself betrayal, degradation, and a suitably painful death by disease. Mrs Linton reserved an even more horrid fate as an awful warning for her suffragette heroine in *The One Too Many* (1894); she marries a policeman, truly a fate worse than the fate worse than death. This attitude was not only confined to women, of course; Henry James's *Daisy Miller* (1879) offers another example. Even the humane Mrs Gaskell exhausted her capacity for daring simply by dealing with an unmarried mother sympathetically in *Ruth* (1853); it was too much that the girl should live and thrive; the offence has to be expiated by suffering, at the close of which she dies, though not quite so gruesomely as the young wife who is only guilty by association with her husband's wild life in *The History of David Grieve* (grieve—grief), which Mrs Humphry Ward published in 1892.

Again and again it is astonishing to realise the ardour with which these women embodied in their fiction the imposed social attitudes of the dominant sex. Women writers were more influential even than men in keeping other women in a carefully defined and rigidly restricted place. To borrow a metaphor from political philosophy, their colonisation by male supremacists was complete; they policed each other. Even the highpowered and fiercely capable Mrs Linton, who felt perfectly confident that any novel of hers could hold its own with *Adam Bede* and *Jane Eyre*, with *East Lynne* thrown in as the ultimate referent, was thrown into paroxysms of submissiveness by the masculine censure of her publisher, Blackwood:

> I am so very sorry you did not like it! Could I not alter it to suit you? Indeed, indeed I am teachable and grateful for criticism, kindly (if not illnaturedly) bestowed, and have very little literary selfwill in the way of holding to my own against the advice of wiser and more experienced people. . . . If I could but interest such a man as yourself I could fear nothing and would gladly farm out my talent to his guidance and to his advantage as well as my own.
>
> (Letter dated April 22 1863, Blackwood MSS, no. 4183, National Library, Edinburgh)

More significant in terms of contemporary events was the

almost universal opposition among these women to female suffrage. All these writers, merely as women, were in the firing-line of the battle of the sexes at its inception. They were all actively involved with the question of woman's role, and their struggles to get to grips with it have a disheartening relevance today. Their work plainly shows the alternating competition with and submission to men, the heart-searchings about marriage as a valid form of union between the sexes, the desperate hunger for education, for function, and the feeling that they should reach and assist other women, which are the major themes of women writers today. But again, like Charlotte, they were feminine but not feminists. No woman writer of any name or distinction threw her weight behind the suffrage struggle (though it is interesting how many of the suffragettes discovered hitherto unsuspected writing skills in the course of the struggle[1]). Most women writers disapproved, Mrs Linton attacking the movement with all the intemperance of her ill-governed nature, and Mrs Humphry Ward proving so effective in the anti-suffrage league that she is personally credited with retarding the emancipation by some years.

Lone voices like that of Olive Schreiner (who, significantly, as a South African, had escaped the standard conditioning of English middle-class girlhood) went unheeded. Her efforts to emphasise the importance of taking each person as unique, of freeing one's perceptions from the inevitable conventional trammels, affected her attitude to life and art as well as politics; but they never enjoyed more than a passing notice. When we are still today bothered by critics who seek to uncover why women write novels, there is a depressing relevance in her rebuke to those who think that "there must be some inherent connection in the human brain between the ovarian sex function and the art of fiction" (*Woman and Labour*); but it was as ineffective then as it is likely to be now.

Occasionally the note of protest against the *status quo* which is to be observed in odd places throughout Victorian women's

---

[1] See, for example, Sylvia Pankhurst's *The Suffragette* (1912), and *The Suffragette Movement* (1931); and we should not forget the names of those who gave as much time and energy to the suffrage movement as they did to their writing, like Isa Craig, Mrs Jameson, Marion Wallace-Dunlop, Lady Morgan, and Harriet Martineau.

writing breaks out into unmistakable bitterness. Mrs Sarah Stickney Ellis, whose *Women of England, Wives of England, Mothers
of England,* and *Daughters of England* were very popular in the
second half of the nineteenth century, maintains a surprisingly
sardonic tone despite the exigencies of her subject-matter and
records this protest against the prevalent conventionalising of
young women's behaviour: "Whatever may be said in novels on
the subject of beauty in tears, seems to be rendered null and void
by the circumstance of marriage having taken place between the
parties" (*The Women of England*, 1839, pp. 225–6). This is a recurrent theme with Mrs Ellis; she feels the impossibility of swim-
ming against the tide, but is determined to have a go at it, writing
of young ladies:

> . . . it seems an ungracious task to attempt to rouse them from their
> summer dream . . . were it not that the cry of utter helplessness
> is of no avail in rescuing from the waters of affliction, and the
> plea of ignorance unheard upon the far-extending and deep ocean
> of experience.
>
> (pp. 17–18)

But there is not much to be built upon the fleeting criticism,
the suppressed complaint. Throughout this period of history the
social standards, and the controls with which to enforce them,
were as rigid and effective as at any point in the extended sweep
of human experience. Small wonder that women laid to their
hearts the only female alternatives as propounded by Ruskin in
*The Ethics of the Dust, Ten Lectures to Little Housewives on the
Elements of Crystallization* (1866), p. 196—"You must be either
house-Wives or house-Moths; remember that. In the deep sense,
you must either weave men's fortunes, and embroider them; or
feed upon, and bring them to decay"—or that "women's rights"
remained "men's lefts", in the meaningless contemporary wit-
ticism.

So far from opening up for women a brave new world, novel-
writing in the nineteenth century was even interpreted as in itself
an ideal way of demonstrating the qualities of female excellence
as defined at that time. Hazel Mews points out how many women
wrote to assist or support their families with the necessary cash,
slaving away devotedly at the literary equivalent of the Song of

The Shirt; others felt it incumbent upon them to display this faculty among their other carefully-acquired "accomplishments"; many more saw the novel as a wonderful opportunity of fulfilling their womanly functions as moral arbiters and guardians of society's standards by producing "conduct books" in a narrative guise; and some, doubtless, saw writing as a thrifty way of filling up their increased leisure in a developing society.

These were, of course, not the only reasons for which women in the nineteenth century wrote novels. George Henry Lewes stated his belief that women novelists wrote to fill an emotional void. His point of view is supported by these poignant remarks, in a letter of 1849, by the bereaved and isolated Charlotte Brontë:

> Lonely as I am—how should I be if Providence had never given me courage to adopt a career—perseverance to plead through two long, weary years with publishers till they admitted me? How should I be with youth past—sisters lost—a resident in a moorland parish where there is not a single educated family? In that case I should have no work at all: the raven, weary of surveying the deluge and without an ark to return to would be my type. As it is, something like a hope and motive sustains me still . . . I wish every woman in England had also a hope and motive: Alas there are many old maids who have neither.

> (*Life, Letters, and Correspondence*, III, 6)

What is really suggested here, however, is that it is not necessarily novel-writing which fills the void, but work. Here again we see how nineteenth-century women stumbled against the restrictions of the age. Writing was the only decent way into the world of work for any woman above the rank of laundress or milliner. But again remarkable is the condescension implied in the asking of the question; Lewes does not trouble to ask why *men* write novels, though they have emotions (and voids) too. It is ironic that try as they might to live up to and propagate the values of the masculine society in which they lived, these women never really shook off their status as curiosities who had to be watched over, accounted for, explained away. So far from being able to establish a truly female tradition of novel-writing in the nineteenth century, these women were, in retrospect, lucky to be able to publish at all. It was doubtless their awareness of this fact which kept them so notably loyal to that sex which had given them their chance in making them the boss-boys of the women's sector.

We cannot reproach them for not being what it was impossible for them to be. We must simply guard against mistaking them for anything other than what they were. Their invaluable contribution to the history of women's writing is that for the first time in the nineteenth century women proved that they could write novels like men. This in itself set an inalienable precedent. It was left to twentieth-century women writers to show that they could write like women.

3

The Writer as Woman in the Twentieth Century

The energies that went into the Regency and Victorian woman's novel today find their outlet in the newspaper article, the television interview, the social investigation; women's novels no longer differ greatly from those of men.

(Hazel Mews, *Frail Vessels*, 1969, p. viii)

No more books. Books all led to the same thing. They were like talking about things. All the things in books were unfulfilled duty. No more interest in men. They shut off the inside world. Women who had anything whatever to do with men were not themselves. They were in a noisy confusion, playing a part all the time.

(The heroine's New Year Resolutions in Dorothy Richardson's *Interim*, 1919, 1938 edition, p. 321)

The discussion about the function and significance of the woman writer which the nineteenth century pursued with such vigour received a radical redefinition in the early decades of the twentieth. Historically speaking, these years brought the first attempt to establish women's writing on its own terms. Many women continued to produce, by the ream, fiction in the old Trollopian mode, as they still do; the Victorian novel has not in any sense perished, but forms the enduring staple of novel-writing even now. However, in the twenties and thirties, the most admired and influential of women writers were seen, and in certain cases saw themselves, as expressing through their work the feminine consciousness, in such a way as to bring out clearly its difference from the male.

Foremost among these in her time was Dorothy Richardson. Her massive *oeuvre, Pilgrimage,* a fluid novel in twelve separate volumes[1] written between 1915 and 1938, shows in its title as well as in themes and structure the interiorisation of the novel which was to be its characteristic development in the twentieth century. It shares with other works of its own age and since the common experience of the spiritual voyage, the search for identity and meaning which is still being conducted, and in very similar metaphors, today—consider Doris Lessing's *Briefing For A Descent Into Hell* (1971). What makes Dorothy Richardson unique is her deliberate attempt to challenge the supremacy of the "masculine" novel of externally observed and authoritative reality by focusing totally on the feminine point of view. Her method, to reduce it to its simplest, consisted of recording the developing consciousness of her heroine in overwhelmingly minute detail over years of her life. The reader is systematically denied the usual fictive sign-posts and guidelines; factual information about the heroine is released spasmodically and piecemeal in order to ensure that we never settle into the cosy sense of "really knowing" the character. Males are only significant in so far as they impinge on the heroine's awareness; there is no effort to present the man's side of events.

Another distinctive feature of Dorothy Richardson's writing is the consistent presence of antimasculine feeling and comment. Partly this proceeds from the author's insistence that her heroine is more important than anyone around her. But there is also quite a positively hostile response to the masculine principle in general. This emerges as an important consideration for women writers of the early twentieth century. They tended on the whole carefully to avoid the overtly feminist posture, displaying, for instance, little interest in suffrage, that cataclysmic struggle which remained unresolved even in 1918, with the restriction of female suffrage to women over thirty. Like George Eliot earlier, they lent moral rather than practical support to the emancipation

[1] The twelve volumes of Dorothy Richardson's *Pilgrimage* are: *Pointed Roofs* (1915), *Backwater* (1916), *Honeycomb* (1917), *The Tunnel* (1918), *Interim* (1919), *Deadlock* (1921), *Revolving Lights* (1923), *The Trap* (1925), *Oberland* (1927), *Dawn's Left Hand* (1931), *Clear Horizon* (1935), and *Dimple Hill* (1938).

movement where they lent anything at all, and it was left to a male writer, Howard Spring, many years later, to attempt to fictionalise the suffragette campaigns in *Fame Is The Spur* (1940). The major women on the literary scene held aloof, and viewed events without much enthusiasm; Virginia Woolf wrote of her most openly feminist book, *Three Guineas* (1938), that it might have more practical value than any of her novels, but that she herself could regard it no higher than as a "good piece of donkey-work", and could not feel for it the emotion that she felt for her novels (*A Writer's Diary*, 1953, p. 288).

But even though there was little strong political consciousness of the executive structures of masculine domination, there was a growing and resentful awareness of the ramifications of social oppression among women at this time. Typical in this respect is Victoria Sackville-West's *All Passion Spent* (1931). A novel without much literary merit, oscillating as it does between the over and underwritten, this book nevertheless touches a central nerve of contemporary thought. Its theme is that of the unfulfilling marriage, but, as the novel makes clear, an empty marriage means a totally wasted life for a woman who is supposed to find her whole life's work within it. The heroine, Lady Slane, has married under the subtle pressures of the man's apparent devotion and her mother's wish to have a daughter well married; the novel begins with his death and traces the heroine's past career through her reminiscences in old age. One by one she becomes awakened to different truths about her history and situation whose cumulative power finally enables her to begin, however belatedly, to live as herself.

An initial disagreeable which has to be overcome is the assumption of the heroine's grown children that as she has depended wholly on their father she will be incapable of self-government. She realises that she has achieved nothing but their contempt as the price of a lifetime's subordination of herself to her husband and family: "Mother had no will of her own. . . . It was assumed that she had not enough brain to be self-assertive. 'Thank goodness,' Herbert sometimes remarked, 'Mother is not one of those clever women'." Looking back it seems to her as if all her life's relationships have been poisoned by the urgent requirement of society that a woman should accomplish her destiny through and within the constraining limits of a man; she comes to see her own mother's role in the marriage as deeply suspect:

> . . . these weeks before the wedding were dedicated wholly to the rites of a mysterious feminism. . . . Matriarchy ruled. Men might have dwindled into insignificance on the planet. Even Henry himself did not count for much. (Yet he was there, terribly there, in the background; and thus, she thought, might a Theban mother have tired her daughter before sending her off to the Minotaur.)
> (p. 158)

Later she extends her anger and bitterness to the whole of her sex:

> Oh, what a pother, she thought, women make about marriage! And yet who can blame them, she added, when one recollects that marriage—and its consequences—is the only thing that women have to make a pother about in the whole of their lives? Although the excitement be vicarious, it will do just as well. Is it not for this function that they have been formed, dressed, bedizened, educated—if so one-sided an affair may be called education—safeguarded, kept in the dark, hinted at, segregated, repressed, all that at a given moment they may be delivered, or may deliver their daughters over, to Minister to a Man?
> (p. 159)

The heroine has made sporadic attempts to break out of the mould. She is not the entirely passive victim that the recurrent use of the sacrificial metaphor might suggest. In her youth she experienced, as the author herself did,[2] subdued sexual fantasies, narcissistic, implicitly lesbian, romantic extravaganzas of "escape and disguise; a changed name, a travestied sex, and freedom in some foreign city"; in her maturity she takes up painting, but is defeated in this by her husband's inability to regard her art as anything but a pastime. She is forced to the conclusion that "he had decoyed her into holding him dearer than her own ambition". As the novel gathers momentum we are led to feel that it is men who are the genuine enemies of women's freedom; other women are merely agents of the masculine social process. The utterly

[2] See Nigel Nicholson's fascinating account of his mother's emotional life, *Portrait of a Marriage* (1973).

conventional good and successful husband Henry is arraigned for his "Jovian detachment and superiority", for his smug self-importance, and for "entering into the general conspiracy to defraud her of her chosen life". Sackville-West is at pains to avoid any suggestion that this is merely an expression of female paranoïa, by creating a male character whose major function is to remind the heroine of all she might have been and done; he tells her at the close, in almost Ibsenish terminology, "Your children your husband, your splendour, were nothing but obstacles that kept you from yourself. They were what you chose to substitute for your real vocation. . . . When you chose that life you sinned against the light. . . ." He clinches the accusation against the husband: "He merely killed you, that's all. Men do kill women" (p. 221).

This is the most condemnatory note sounded in the course of the novel, and the advice comes too late for the heroine to profit from it. Nor does the novelist have any intention of allowing her heroine to develop into a St Joan of S.W.1 The note of feminist protest is consistently sounded only to be immediately muted; each passage of complaint is followed by some inhibition such as this:

> Yet she was no feminist. She was too wise a woman to indulge in such luxuries as an imagined martyrdom. The rift between herself and life was not the rift between man and woman, but the rift between the worker and the dreamer. That she was a woman, and Henry a man, was really a matter of chance. She would go no further than to acknowledge that the fact of her being a woman made the situation a degree more difficult.
>
> (p. 164)

The heroine's inability to complete the analysis of her situation in any constructive way has meant that she has never known how to change it. One by one she closes up the doors of her soul and merges into the life framed for her by, successively, parents, husband, and children. The writer shows clearly how this sort of woman is always somebody's property and responsibility, and never her own: "She remembered acquiescing in the assumption that she should project herself into the lives of her children." Such relationships are not necessarily based on love; freed by the death of Henry, she is able to escape the final course of the typical destiny, dependence upon children. She owns to herself at last the dislike she feels for her offspring, and shrugs them off like old shoes. But this is the full extent of her revolt. Lady Slane does not progress beyond the reaction characteristic of the well-bred young girl, to want the victory without the fight, the change without the unrest. She wants to be free without shaking off the oppressor, she wants her own way without having to contradict someone else's. This is made explicit in an important central section, in which Vita Sackville-West returns again to the "woman question":

> Was there, after all, some foundation for the prevalent belief that woman should minister to man? Had the generations been right, the personal struggle wrong? Was there something beautiful, something active, something creative even, in her apparent submission to Henry? . . . Was this not also an achievement of the sort peculiarly suited to women? of the sort, indeed, which women alone could compass; a privilege, a prerogative, not to be despised? All the woman in her answered, yes! All the artist in her countered, no!
>
> And then again, were not women in their new Protestant spirit defrauding the world of some poor remnant of enchantment, some illusion, foolish perhaps, but lovely? This time the woman and artist in her alike answered, yes.

(pp. 175–6)

So much for the feminist revolution; women must stay as they are. As this suggests, there is some sympathy for the heroine, but the novel's orientation is undoubtedly masculine. The feminist theme is used, exploited even, to trick out what is basically an inferior romance, masquerading as a serious piece of fiction. The writer lets herself off most of the challenges of the subject. There is no attempt, for instance, to consider the difficulties of ordinary women; Lady Slane's life is only adjudged wasted because she had an artistic talent, and the implication is that marriage is a perfectly suitable repository for the ungifted female. Again, the "free" Lady Slane does nothing more outrageous than take a flat away from her children. She is too old and frail to recapture anything except a little winter sun. There is no pain in her story; it is all tastefully softened into old age and the message is lost in a geriatric twilight.

There were, however, other ways than this of making a mark as a woman writer in the thirties. One woman above all seemed to her contemporaries to be the writer who discerned "the peculiar nature of typically feminine modes of thought and apprehension, and their peculiar value as the complement of masculine modes" (Joan Bennett, *Virginia Woolf, Her Art as a Novelist*, 1945, pp. 76–7). Virginia Woolf has long been regarded as epitomising the spirit of "Bloomsbury", and the literary temper of the period. There is a sense in which she must also be regarded as the archetypal "woman writer" as well. Looking back on the great myth-making decades of the Twenties and Thirties, whose effects we are even now struggling to identify, let alone free ourselves from, it seems in retrospect as if the quintessentially male writer of the Lawrence/Hemingway type was evolving by contrast with the essential woman writer. Both then and now Virginia Woolf both created and fitted into the received impression of the woman writer which has been little affected through the years by the achievements of robuster geniuses like George Eliot. Moody, intuitive, alert to detail, and constantly suffering and expressing her feminine sensibility, she has come to hold a position in some quarters of literary history which would have filled her with disdain. It is almost as if, in those prepotent years, novelist and novel were apprehended as one reality; the novelist male or female at this time seems to have been more than usually subject to the vulgar fallacy of the confusion between writer and work. Novel equals self in the common awareness of both Lawrence and Woolf—male and female self, that is.

Virginia Woolf was herself keenly alive to the difficulties of writing as a woman in her time:

> . . . I found, directly I put pen to paper, you cannot review even a novel without having a mind of your own, without expressing what you take to be the truth about human relations, morality, sex. And all these questions, according to the Angel of the House, cannot be dealt with freely and openly by women; they must charm, they must conciliate, they must—to put it bluntly—tell lies. [This is] a real experience; it was an experience that was bound to befall all women writers at that time. Killing the Angel in the house was part of the occupation of a woman writer.
>
> (*The Death of the Moth*, p. 151)

73

This diagnosis of the operation in literature and criticism, as well as in society at large, of sex-based beliefs and expectations, has proved unerringly accurate. She has herself, perhaps more than any other woman writer, been haunted by critical consciousness of her sex. David Daiches' sense of her as a woman writer is nowhere modified by his knowledge of the disdain with which his subject regarded the idea: he wrote in *Virginia Woolf* (1945), p. 145, "there can be little question that she was the greatest woman novelist of her time, though she herself would have objected to the separation of her sex implied in such a judgment"; and like other critics of her work he keeps her sex firmly before the reader by referring to her as "Mrs Woolf" throughout. By other critics she is supposed to illustrate through her female characters "essential womanliness"; this again must surely be critical projection of an acquaintance with her own nature and characteristics?

She was, in her life, limited largely to one social sphere, and to a very small range of moral and intellectual types. This resulted, among other things, in the fact that she never tried to treat any other than women of her own quality in any depth. Women of action in general, and feminists in particular, are shown to be comic (though as we have seen, she was not out of sympathy with the movement, treating it favourably in *A Room of One's Own* as well as in *Three Guineas*). In addition Virginia Woolf positively hated "common" women, lapsing into her most unoriginal, conventional "character-sketch" type of writing in dealing with, say, Mrs Haines in *Between The Acts* (1941). Even her admirers sometimes feel as if the light of her imaginative comprehension only plays upon the educated and sensitive, the social, moral, and aesthetic élite; and are we really to accept that only in the females of this caste is "essential womanliness" to be found?

Virginia's famous "sensitivity" seems to dog her almost like a bad name, especially in these days of what Mary Ellman has called "warty-lad novelists". But it is more complex than an everyday manifestation of a female mode of feeling. Her superfine awareness of every grain in the texture of living, her presentation of her characters as raw to life and experience, spring in part from her own defensive paranoia: "I am alone in a hostile world. The human face is hideous. This is to my liking" (*The Waves*, 1931, p. 113). Although aware of the pitfalls confronting characters whom she makes react like this, Virginia Woolf nonetheless asks us to empathise with them. Many readers are unfortunately repelled by what seems to be the very clearly defined class-consciousness of her main subjects; attitudes like Neville's "I cannot read in the presence of horse-dealers and plumbers" (p. 51) appear to exemplify that mixture of intellectual and social snobbishness which its detractors see as the essence of "Bloomsbury".

But a closer look at the whole passage makes it plain that Neville's disgust with his travelling companions is not really that, as lower orders, "they will make it impossible for me always to read Catullus in a third-class railway carriage". It springs from his desperate conviction that "we are all pellets". Latterday champions of horse-dealers and plumbers should note that Neville is much harder on himself than on them; contemplating his own future he concludes "It would be better to breed horses and live in one of those red villas than to run in and out of the skulls of Sophocles and Euripides like a maggot, with a high-minded wife, one of those University women". A feminist critic might observe the routine belittling of intelligent women, even, as here, by an intelligent woman, but would also have to concede that the men do not come off so well, either; there is an unmistakable trace of antipathy to the masculine principle in Virginia Woolf's "sensitivity".

In part this is a legacy of Cranford conventions—men have big boots and loud voices. Further, there is always in Virginia Woolf the slight shudder of aesthetic disdain felt towards male characters who are physically or mentally unattractive (think of the wretched Tansley in *To The Lighthouse*, 1927, and compare this treatment with the kindness always shown by Jane Austen towards plain men and women—even the rebarbative Mr Collins in *Pride and Prejudice* gets off remarkably lightly). Virginia Woolf's fiction similarly inhabits a world of minute social and personal gradations, but as the writer is without Jane Austen's fine sense of character and circumstance, and variety of flexible techniques, by which she demonstrates to us and proves that her judgments are right, the tendency is for Virginia Woolf's writing to appear to be the expression of the pervasive élitism of her own personal life, projected untreated, as it were, on to the page. She was herself alive to the limitations of her own talent and method:

> I think I have got at a more direct method of summarising relations; and then the poems (in metre) ran off the prose lyric vein, which, as I agree with Roger, I overdo. That was, by the way, the best criticism I've had for a long time: that I poetise my inanimate scenes, stress my personality; don't let the meaning emerge from the matière.
>
> (*A Writer's Diary*, p. 311)

Another element of Virginia Woolf's antimasculine feeling arises not so much from sensitivity as from fear. The judgment which rejects with distaste the man who is short, ignorant, or graceless, is in fact deriving its axis from an intimidatingly high standard of masculine superiority which recalls the Renaissance concept of all-round excellence. Thus we are told, *tout court*, that Mr Ramsay in *To The Lighthouse* is "the greatest metaphysician of the time", when the height of his performance in that line is represented by the reflection that "the very stone one kicks with one's boot will outlast Shakespeare", and by the empty rhetoric of "Does the progress of civilisation depend upon great men?" There are occasions on which he is touched by authorial irony; now and then his position in the novel is undercut as his self-assessment is shown to be overrated and his behaviour as a consequence absurd:

> He shivered, he quivered. All his vanity, all his satisfaction in his own splendour, riding fell as a thunderbolt, fierce as a hawk at the head of his men through the valley of death, had been shattered, destroyed. Stormed at by shot and shell, boldly we rode and well, flashed through the valley of death, volleyed and thundered—straight into Lily Briscoe and William Bankes. He quivered; he shivered.
>
> (p. 52)

But this is not characteristic of the presentation of Ramsay as a whole. He is a threatening figure of power and drive; his ego-needs dominate the novel, and his progress forms its structure, though many critics assume that the book is "about" his wife. Although like most successful men he lives almost entirely apart from his wife and family, his personality operating among them is a major influence upon their lives. They dread, with reason, the irruption of his presence; we are mainly introduced to him in the early section of the novel through the apprehension of his wife and son. And as the echo of *The Charge of the Light Brigade* in his thoughts above makes clear, he is subliminally compelled by ideas of war, strife, and suffering. He is driven to express his aggression at times, regardless of the effect on Mrs Ramsay:

> To pursue truth with such astonishing lack of consideration for other people's feelings, to rend the veils of civilisation so wantonly, so brutally, was to her so horrible an outrage of human decency that, without replying, dazed and blinded, she bent her head as if to let the pelt of jagged hail, the drench of dirty water, bespatter her unrebuked. There was nothing to be said.
>
> (p. 54)

Readers unfamiliar with the world of Woolf, but reared on *Last Exit to Brooklyn* or *The Naked Lunch* may be surprised to learn that the husband's offence is to have said "Damn you"— also that within seconds of Mr Ramsay's retraction of the curse, his wife has subsided once more into her ill-founded but compulsive attitude of reverential submission: "She was not good enough to tie his shoe strings, she felt." Nor is it only in his authority role that Mr Ramsay is frightening. He plays an important part in the sexual structure of the novel. Sexual themes are, characteristically, treated very allusively indeed in Virginia Woolf, approached (when at all) via the metaphor, under cover of the symbol. The strong sexual undercurrent to much of her writing has not so far been fully investigated; but we may note the very precise sexual symbolism of Mr Ramsay's "blade", as well as of the general associating of him with war and weapons. Linked with his father's sexual tensions is the small son James, who is growing by degrees into more and more of Mrs Ramsay's langorous, almost erotic tenderness—the boy's fascination with the dangerous flashing scissors (given Virginia's love of and familiarity with classical Greek) surely represents an allusion to the castration myth of Cronos and Uranus? Other characters too are woven into the sexual scheme of the novel; any post-Freudian will recognise the significance of Cam's alternating hostility and love, while Mrs Ramsay's very special relationships with men, followed by her sudden swift death, recalls the ancient dance of *eros* and *thanatos* which has been conducted time out of mind. Consider, too, the elegiac treatment of the loss of Minta's "jewel", her maiden state; there is a genuine mourning and sense of bereavement here. But Mr Ramsay it is who despite his complete lack of obvious sexuality conveys the novel's main sexual charge, representing as he does the masculine principle of vengeful authority.

This kind of sensitivity to the implications and abrasions of personal relationships also strongly marked the work of another female writer of this period; indeed, it is so much a characteristic of women's writing in the early decades of the twentieth century that the reader may wonder if it was catching. Katherine Mansfield was so ill for so much of her mature productive phase that it is unfair to suggest that her delicacy arose simply from "nerves". Nevertheless, the feeling expressed here pervaded her fiction as her life:

> Yesterday was simply hellish for me. My work went very well, but all the same, I suffered abominably. I felt so alien and far away, and everybody cheated me, everybody was ugly and beyond words cruel.
>
> (*Katherine Mansfield's Letters to John Middleton Murry 1913–1922*, 1951, p. 38)

Again and again this note recurs; "Everybody is too big—too crude—too ugly" (pp. 200–1). This exaggerated sensibility is only part of Katherine Mansfield's disturbed personality. Throughout her life she was unsure, fundamentally, of her sexual and personal identity. At times she accepted her dependence on Middleton Murry for her writing; at others she became aggressive and dominating, pure "masculine" ego. Beneath it all however lurked in her the motherless child—"Talk to ME. I'm lonely, I haven't ONE single soul" (*Letters*, p. 597). As a person she alternated constantly between female and male, adult and child. But as a writer she almost invariably subordinates men to women and children in her stories. Does she then "play the man" with her brainchildren as she claims to have had to do with Middleton Murry?

Both Virginia Woolf and Katherine Mansfield pose the question of the nature of the creative process in women writers. Virginia Woolf's admirers may point enthusiastically to her mastery of the new technique of impersonal subjectivism, her destruction of the hegemony of exterior reality, and will feel that her method of multipersonal representation does in fact achieve the synthesis which is its aim. But detractors will continue to insist that she merely "poetises" her *own* self, and has no power to grasp the felt existence of another individual. This is expressed by D. S. Savage: ". . . she lacked the first requirements of a good novelist: the ability to create living, credible characters whose life is projected into an interesting and significant narrative pattern" (*The Withered Branch*, 1950, p. 71). In much the same way Katherine Mansfield habitually went inward rather than out in her search for material, summing up her two motives for writing as "joy—real joy" and "*a cry against corruption*" (*Letters*, p. 149). She was aware of the need to lend credibility to the characters surrounding the central figure who carries the main weight of the fiction's thematic burden, writing to Sylvia Lind:

> I find my great difficulty in writing is to learn to submit. Not that one ought to be without resistance—of course I don't mean that. But when I am writing of "another I want so to lose myself in the soul of the other that I am not . . ."
>
> (Ruth Elvish Mantz, *The Critical Bibliography of Katherine Mansfield*, 1931, p. 193)

But it is interesting that she expresses her approach to the craft of writing in intensely emotional terms, almost as an act of love; and interesting too that she instinctively uses the "female" metaphor of submission to describe what has traditionally been regarded as the "masculine" act of shaping and constructing. As my argument has so far suggested, these distinctions are not accurate or helpful; but there can be little doubt that the work of Dorothy Richardson, Virginia Woolf, and Katherine Mansfield has contributed substantially to the impression that women's writing consists in the main of the heightened subjective, with a heavy reliance upon the minutiae of living: "Do you, too, feel an infinite delight and value in *detail*—not for the sake of detail but for the life in the life of it?" (Mantz, p. 183).

Inevitably there had to be a reaction. Women writers in these years may have deliberately avoided the feminist posture as too sectarian and constricting, tying the artist too tightly to the concerns of one segment of society in one short epoch. But as the history of the century has shown, the consciously feminine was also fated to enjoy a relatively brief life-span. First, the form itself proved to be of limited validity, workable only by a few, and cut off from the main flow of the novel's evolution, a side stream leading nowhere. Mary McCarthy makes this point: "Even when it is most serious, the novel's characteristic tone is one of gossip and tittle-tattle . . . if the breath of scandal has not touched it, the book is not a novel. That is the trouble with the art-novel (most of Virginia Woolf, for instance); it does not stoop to gossip" (*On The Contrary*, pp. 264–5). Then, too, even in her own age there were those who objected to Virginia Woolf's purpose and techniques; D. S. Savage led the pack who felt that "her method was one of retraction rather than extension—a narrowing of focus to take in only that which readily lent itself to appropriation by her extraordinarily limited vision" (p. 79).

Those critics who judge, as Savage did, exclusively by the standards of the old-fashioned "well-made" Victorian novel, as safe and comfortable as an old four-poster bed, will be out of sympathy with Virginia Woolf's efforts to create a new novel mode which she tentatively called an "elegy". But even sympathetic fellow-travellers like Rosamond Lehmann observe that "blinds sway, brooms tap, chairs creak too frequently". To some extent, too, there has been in recent years a fashionable backlash against the social and intellectual conventions of that time, and many modern readers feel cowed by Virginia Woolf's classically cultured background, extensive reading, and mandarin assumptions. Her "sensitivity" appears to rebuke our coarseness; her strictures on the vulgarity of the Edwardian novel (*The Common Reader*, 1925, p. 184ff.), her famous placing witticisms, and her belief that "an ordinary mind on an ordinary day" can feel the swift supple responses that she describes, all proclaim her finer than normal emotional and intellectual capacities. Finally there is her insistence that all experience, no matter how casual, has the luminous quality which she refers to throughout her fictional and critical writing. The reader may feel that he gets no respite. He can be made to feel common indeed.

It may be too late even to attempt to overturn this impression of Virginia Woolf, but it cannot be passed over without remark. First, there is a complete distortion of her character in the picturing of Virginia as an old prune, in the omission of her relish of life, her sense of humour, her enchanting gaiety, her love of new experience and her ability to adapt to it. This first-person anecdote, in Quentin Bell's admirable *Virginia Woolf: A Biography* (1972), I, 124, gives some idea of the Virginia that we hardly ever see:

> Suddenly the door opened and the long and sinister figure of Mr Lytton Strachey stood on the threshold. He pointed his finger at a stain on Vanessa's white dress.
> "Semen?" he said.
> Can one really say it? I thought & we burst out laughing. With that one word all barriers of reticence and reserve went down. A flood of the sacred fluid seemed to overwhelm us. Sex permeated our conversation. The word bugger was never far from our lips. We discussed copulation with the same excitement and openness that we had discussed the nature of good.

Then, too, any reader who slinks away from what he takes to be the imposing shade, will be denying himself the acquaintance of one of our greatest, most distinctive writers. The fine feeling, the linguistic dexterity, the attention to detail, combine in the work of Virginia Woolf to produce moments of a piercing sweetness that are not to be found elsewhere outside the lyric vein of Shakespeare. These usually consist of transient moods, fleeting experiences, the sense of the ephemeral sharpened by her awareness of the ever-present eternal. Through stressing what passes away, she enables us to grasp what remains; and she succeeds, repeatedly, in evoking the presence of beauty, grace, and love. Pity then the reader who, fearing to encounter what Norman Mailer has sneeringly called a "lady-book", turns away from the novels of Virginia Woolf.

There has been, in fact, little overt masculine protest against this "feminisation" of the novel. Many of the keenest admirers of these women writers were men, and inevitably they depended largely on men for their start in publishing, short-story writing, journalism and so on. Leon Edel comments wryly "I had noted the extent to which some of the male members of my Princeton seminar had actually resented being manœuvred by Dorothy Richardson into the mind of an adolescent girl" (p. 71); and both Virginia Woolf and Katherine Mansfield have been known to provoke feelings akin to Lucky Jim's classic response to Margaret, the desire to push a bead up her nose. But on the whole male objections where they came did not come with any discernible misogynist basis.

At all events, posterity disposes regardless of such considerations. Virginia Woolf has survived throughout this century, and her reputation is as secure now as it was in her lifetime; and Katherine Mansfield is assured of her small cult following, which will surely increase as a result of the serialisation of her life and stories (together, as a continuum, interestingly enough) by the B.B.C. in 1973. But Dorothy Richardson's once massive reputation has now so far faded that a recent study of her had to be subtitled "Unknown genius", and writers like Elizabeth Bowen had to witness in the second half of their lives the irreversible erosion of the fame which they had spent their early years building up. Time, rather than man, has been the enemy in these cases.

So much, then, for the "feminine" novel. Virginia Woolf and others undoubtedly succeeded in creating a distinctively feminine style—not that this necessarily prevented men from essaying it —but it is much more difficult to make out a case for the establishing of any continuing feminine tradition. Like all splendidly great and original writers, all that Virginia Woolf could offer to other writers following on was a literary impasse. She was, too, fully aware herself how much her success derived from her having been able to achieve something very much nearer to a man's life than a woman's, declaring for what was, in contemporary terms, a masculine ideal, the freedom and privacy of a *man* of letters, as an essential prerequisite: "A woman must have money and a room of her own if she is to write fiction" (*A Room Of One's Own*, p. 6).

In this, as in so much else, she was untypical both of her time and her sex. The unique crystalline style in life and art is memorable and impressive, but cannot readily be emulated. It is worth noticing in passing that very few women writers have ever had either of these aids to creation which she insisted on; financial independence and privacy at will are not so easily come by for anybody, and have not been felt as female needs, even by women themselves. We smile at James Austen-Leigh's account of his famous aunt Jane scribbling away at a desk in the family sitting-room, alert for the creak of the hall door which was her signal to slip her papers unobtrusively together; we admire Mrs Gaskell's domestic management as she wrote on the dining-room table from a seat which commanded, through three open doors, views of different areas of her house; we feel aggrieved with Katherine Mansfield in her regular discovery that wherever and whenever she set up house with Middleton Murry, he automatically took possession of the study while she was relegated to the kitchen table, or left forgotten at the sink doing dishes. But do we ever stop to wonder how under such circumstances these women writers produced anything at all, let alone work of sustained quality and quantity? Mrs Humphry Ward seems fortunate in comparison in being able to share the study of her enlightened husband—and it is only very recently, where at all, that women's writing has justified itself in terms of external requirements on the same lines as that of men.

What then is the situation of the twentieth-century woman writer, seen against the background of her historical struggle to make her contribution to art, even if only in this one form? Certain features emerge fairly obviously as key factors in the success of those who have done so. It seems just to say, for instance, that the traditional Anglo-Saxon culture of female subordination effected first through paternal domination and later through married life and the exclusion from work, has been inimical to women's literary achievement. In the modern period especially it is interesting to observe how many of our distinguished women writers bring to their fiction something apart from the "English rose" girlhood and upbringing. Like Olive Schreiner before her, Doris Lessing is very evidently South African, while Edna O'Brien and Iris Murdoch have in common the strain of Irish blood (though happily the strain is telling only upon one of them). Muriel Spark unites elements of Jewish and Scottish, Katherine Mansfield was from New Zealand. In the case of the immigrant women writers in particular, the throwing-off of the background was a vital part of their development as artists, even when it only provided the perspective of distance sufficient to enable that background to be lovingly fictionalised, as in Katherine Mansfield's case.

Marriage on the whole constitutes a threat to women writers, perhaps because in the nature of the institution women have been tacitly (and sometimes noisily) required to surrender that autonomy which is essential to the practice of any art. In this case singularity is usually blessed; we are reminded of the advice given by a childless woman to a girl who chooses a single poet's life rather than a married woman's in Ivy Compton-Burnett's *Men and Wives*: "A selfish life is a lovely life, darling." There must have been many women who suffered a spiritual death, as Charlotte Brontë a physical, with the advent of marriage and all its consequences. It is not only a masculine fate to be a "mute inglorious Milton". Zelda Fitzgerald is a case in point here. She wrote all her life, and particularly in her youth was a tireless diarist and letter-writer. It is only recently that Nancy Milford, in *Zelda Fitzgerald: A Biography* (1970), has drawn attention to the extent of Scott Fitzgerald's plagiarising of his wife's writings. Understandably or not, he regarded their entire life together as "his" material, and felt that her attempt to fictionalise part of it in her only novel, *Save Me The Waltz*, was an unscrupulous descent and a betrayal of the meaning of their life together. It was this act of Zelda, rather than the infidelity which the novel celebrates, that brought about the final death of Scott's love. Scott also felt passionately that the flowering of whatever talent his wife possessed was due entirely to her debt to *"the greenhouse of my money, and my name, and my love"* (p. 271). Comparisons are pointless, and who could wish to sacrifice anything that Scott himself wrote in favour of some hypothetical contribution from Zelda? But other women writers have been more fortunate in their choice of the matrimonial greenhouse, and it is suggestive of the continuous willed disaster of Zelda's life that having some literary talent of her own, she tried to bloom in the "greenhouse" kept by the most distinguished writer of their entire generation.

When they have married, women writers have tended towards men who have loved and served their geniuses, who have been able to accept constructively and on the whole gracefully the surbordinate role; "Mr Siddons". Otherwise the marriage has proved less durable than the woman's talent (though writers as different as Dorothy Parker and Carson McCullers divorced and then remarried men who could live neither with nor without their clever wives). On at least one occasion the man proved to be the midwife to the woman's talent; George Henry Lewes certainly assisted George Eliot, to put it no higher, towards the definitive expression of her varied gifts as well as lending her his first name, and Edmund Wilson is similarly credited with directing Mary McCarthy's transition from criticism to fiction, reputedly by locking her up till she had done something "creative". As this apocryphal story suggests, the element of Svengali is not entirely absent (as how could it be, all things considered?). Virginia Woolf dreaded what she called the "beak" of Leonard's critical comment, but awaited his verdict on all her new productions as among the most important of all the opinions she was likely to receive; she invariably sought not only his advice but also relied on his practical help with the revising, editing, and even punctuation of her work.

It is hardly coincidental too that among women writers often the greatest and most distinctive have been childless: Jane Austen, the three Brontës, George Eliot, Virginia Woolf, Ivy Compton-Burnett, Iris Murdoch, Stevie Smith. Amongst others a picture of relative childlessness comes through, women writers tending to limit their child-bearing more than has been customary, where they could not avoid it altogether (Katherine Mansfield, despite the oft-repeated sentimentalism about her longing for children, miscarried of her first pregnancy through an "accident" while heaving a heavy trunk from a high wardrobe, and used her faithful friend L.M.'s savings to abort her second[3]). This does not invariably follow. Margaret Drabble has stated that for her, physical and mental creativity are linked; she wrote her first, second, and third novels while awaiting the birth of her first, second, and third children. But hers would seem to be a special case; the hand that rocks the cradle may have little energy left for pounding the typewriter, and in this, as in other respects, it has so

[3] See, for an account of this hitherto undisclosed incident, the fascinating and moving *Katherine Mansfield: The Memories of L.M.*, pp. 64–5.

far at least been necessary for women to emulate men, as far as their physiology allows.

These then are the disadvantages of the woman's life. It is not, though, a picture of unrelieved misery, frustration and enslavement. There have been suggestions that certain aspects of a woman's life were positively conducive to novel-writing. Virginia Woolf expressed it like this:

> . . . all the literary training that a woman had in the early nineteenth century was training in the observation of character, in the analysis of emotion. Her sensibility had been educated for centuries by the influence of the common sitting-room. People's feelings were impressed on her, personal relations were always before her eyes.

> (*A Room Of One's Own*, p. 100)

Margaret Drabble again has made a similar point about the twentieth century; women, she feels, have plenty of experience of daily life, and "novels are about daily life". This links with the widespread assumption that women, more than men, rely on the basis of disguised autobiography in their writing (is it too naïve to point out that men have "daily lives" too?). It is a tendency deliberately played upon by Mary McCarthy when she declared herself to be the sexually adventurous heroine of her short story, "The Man In The Brooks Brothers Shirt".

Plainly the writer's own lived and felt everyday experience will form the inalienable matrix of creation. Why assume, though, as so much comment seems to, that the process occurs only in women? Take Doris Lessing's account, in the very largely autobiographical *Martha Quest*, of how Martha embarks on her career as a writer:

> For a few days then she dreamed of herself as a writer. She would be a free lance. She wrote poems, lying on the floor of her room; an article on the monopoly press; and a short story about a young girl who. . . . This story was called "Revolt".

> (Part Four, Chapter Two)

Has literature no examples of male writers who began their work with stories about a young man who. . . ? We need think no further than the portraits of artists as young man and young dog delineated by James Joyce and Dylan Thomas; and there is always

Proust to quash any suggestion that women have better memories for detail than men. Writers have better memories than ordinary people; that is all.

There remains, however, the theory that women writers are those who have succeeded in turning certain potentially restrictive aspects of their lives to advantage. Margaret Drabble has claimed that it is easier for a woman, freed from the tyranny of economic necessity to work and provide which cramps the lives of most men, to find or make the time to write. She has also, like other women, stressed the point made by Virginia Woolf that it is a cheap and unobtrusive career to launch oneself on. Certainly we know that several women who have won world-wide respect as writers originally contemplated other art forms as the vehicle for their talents; Carson McCullers for many years subordinated her writing to a deep commitment to music, and others tried their hand at painting; this is described, again by Doris Lessing in *Martha Quest* (IV, 2), with the irony of hindsight (note the echo of Virginia Woolf):

> She remembered that as a child she had had a talent for drawing. She made a sketch there and then of the view of the park from her door; it really wasn't too bad at all. But the difficulty with being a painter is that one must have equipment. Ah, the many thousands of hopeful young writers there are, for no better reason than that a pencil and writing pad takes up less room than an easel, paints, and drawing boards, besides being so much less expensive.

Arguably the urge to paint is not strong here. The young Martha is rather struck with the notion of "being a painter" than driven by the compulsion to express herself in *this* medium and no other, which presumably motivated impoverished youngsters who began, as most of the great painters did, with nothing. Martha is, too, drawn with resentful urgency simply to claim for herself what she sees as the "masculine" free life of the artist; her use of the masculine image of the free "lance" is significant; particularly as this ideal is defined in Martha's instance by comparison with the especially odious and restricted life of the South African white woman.

But perhaps there is something of wider application to all women writers in the settling for less which is recorded here.

Could it be that this process, so characteristic of the female psyche in some of its manifestations, is responsible for the generalised underachievement of women across the whole of the artistic spectrum? Or is it due to the consciousness of masculine prejudice which makes women stick to something that they can hide under their embroidery if need be? Virginia Woolf insisted that creative women are always "impeded by the extreme conventionality of the other sex". We should probably widen this to interpret it as a general social prejudice, rather than an exclusively masculine one, and again it would seem that nonconformist men have had as much to put up with from philistines and conformists as women have. But there still remains the irreducible difference between a man's life and a woman's, between the contribution of men to the various art forms, and that of women. How is the feminist critic to come to terms with these facts?

It seems to me that women's contribution to art must be assessed in relation to their opportunities as a sex, which at best have usually been, and remain, inferior to the best offered to men. Criticism is inclined to treat each new generation of women writers as if they were the first in the field, but those women who could write, always did. Paradoxically in view of the harshly antifeminist temper of the Middle Ages, the Paston women whose letters so well reveal their literary as well as their commercial and human abilities, were better off than any of their male serfs, in this respect. Women wrote, as men did, in the contemporarily available literary modes, with an inevitable bias towards that currently prevailing, again like the men. It is not so much writing habits which have altered to admit women into the literary arena by way of the novel, but educational and social. As society evolved from the medieval period, aristocratic women tended to lose that educational advantage that had accrued to them at a time when education as a whole was almost totally class-based in its distribution. Nor were they advantaged by the cultural development of the nineteenth century which partly replaced class by sex as the criterion for the receipt of educational opportunity, through the establishing of the public schools. Opportunity is a fine thing, as the proverb assures us, and so many women simply never received theirs.

Nevertheless, a century of free compulsory public education, together with the increasing flexibility of society, has had its effect. It cannot explain why women writers took to the novel with such astonishing aptitude in the very early years of the nineteenth century. But it is important to spare at least a passing thought for all the millions of underprivileged men, and to recall that at the time when women were first establishing themselves as writers in any numbers during the late nineteenth and early twentieth centuries, when they seemed to be bursting into the hitherto charmed literary circles with more vigour than becoming modesty, more men were too. The rapid advances in education, and the thrustful upsurge of an expanding culture and economy, threw into prominence many men who in all likelihood would otherwise have achieved no greater fame than that of being the local ancient mariner—we may call this the H. G. Wells syndrome. Why do more women write novels than anything else? The answer to this surely lies somewhere in terms of the fact that more people write novels than anything else.

Still, it is often tacitly accepted (usually by those of us who have never tried it) that novels are easier than anything else to write. We are all said to have a novel in us, rather than a poem or a play. Perhaps this is connected with the association of women writers with the novel; many feminist commentators have asserted that the low status accorded to women affects adversely the evaluation of all forms, activities, and occupations that they are involved with. Is there any feeling that writing novels simply must be easier if so many women can do? Nowadays novel-writing is often the intelligent housewife's version of pottery classes or flower arranging, something done to keep busy and improve herself while the husband is at work. It is considerably belittling to the efforts of professional women writers that the colour supplements so delight in informing their impressionable readers that a certain woman, whose principal function appears to be to decorate the social scene, or to prop up a high-achieving husband, is also, in her spare time, "working on a novel".

But the category itself, of "woman writer", however useful a term of description, is ultimately a down-grading mechanism. It cannot be made to serve much worthwhile critical purpose, for it is not possible to show that women writers have anything in common with each other as a group. We cannot, for instance, say that all women, as writers, lack humour, energy, or the ability to create character, even if this charge can be hung (unjustly) on one individual like Virginia Woolf. It cannot be proved that "women writers" display more personal and social tensions, that they resort more to what Raymond Williams called "the fiction of special pleading", even though Charlotte Brontë does. It is not evident that they avoid the "masculine" authority mode of the third-person narrative and the omniscient view, or the creation of male characters, or the use of the male as the authorial mouthpiece or presence in the novel. The developing of the "feminine" novel in the early twentieth century did not inhibit the continuance of the senior "masculine" form, which marches on today. What then is the point of using the term "woman writer"?

It could equally well be asked if there is any point in arguing against it. It will obviously continue to be used, if only as a useful pigeonhole, for dons as well as journalists. But the aim of criticism ought to be rather higher than that of simple classification of authors by sex. Basically this phrase is pejorative in its implication that women can and should be split off from the main body of writers to be studied apart. Compare it with other such trivialising subsections: regional novelist, Northern writer, dialect poet, poetess. Its absurdity is revealed if we simply match "lady novelist", a phrase still in use, with "gentlemen novelist", or compare "woman writer" with "man writer". For most women, creative or not, the fundamental choice, where the woman is enabled to raise her consciousness sufficiently to make it, is between sex and self, in Betty Friedan's phrase. Does she choose, that is, to live within her sex, undergoing all the personal, social, and educational restrictions that that can entail, or does she make the bid for full selfhood and equal partnership in human affairs?

For the artist, of either sex, the choice is between various modes, certain of which, for convenience, we may call "masculine" or "feminine", though these are not exclusively monopolised by, and may indeed have little direct relation to, individual beings of either sex. Nor can the creative choice be even as clear-cut as this. Like all its members, the artist can only survive within society by accepting many, if not all, of its sexually-determined stereotypes and agreed behavioural differences. This endorsement is bound to be reflected in his art. But recent research on the novel by Mark Schorer and Karl Kroeber has clarified the extent to which the tone of a work is dictated not by the developed attitudes of the writer, but by the matrix of related images thrown up by the subconscious assumptions implicit in the operation of verbalising. Consequently, where the writer or critic falls into adopting the associations inherent even in the half-conscious use of the category, there is inevitably involved a diminishing of the full artist, the full human being, and one may feel, the full reader too.

Accepting that it is not possible simply to demolish the terminology of classification, it is my feeling that we should resist its encroachment upon our critical processes, even if we do not agree with the advanced feminist thinkers of today who teach that "woman" is used as a mark of irreversible inferiority of status, to denote the substandard or to serve as a covert term of abuse. The primary objection to the blanket use of the concept must be that it facilitates the adoption of just such rigid postures as this, by releasing irrational and emotional associations into the critical atmosphere like a swarm of gnats; the response on learning that a writer is a man or woman has been compared with that which obtains on being informed of another's political convictions.

Like politics, sex is an inevitable factor of human existence, and an endlessly fascinating one. Hence sex-based critical modes and the widespread use of sexual analogy are probably not only inevitable likewise, but also necessary to aid us in our never-ending struggle to impose some significant distinctions upon the resistless flux of experience. But what we can and I think should endeavour to do is to sharpen our awareness of these figures within our shaping consciousness so that we may free ourselves from the unhelpful reductive generalisation. Art and criticism alike find their primary work in the making of distinctions; but there is also a vital sense in which the naming of anything alienates it from its true self, diminishes its capacity by refusing to recognise its uniqueness, and renders it easier for society's consumption by asserting control over its essential individuality. It is my contention that something of this sort occurs every time we use the phrase "woman writer"; that it is, finally, the uncomprehending assault of the outsider on the lonely mystery of the solitary artist.

4

Sexual Themes

A story must be exceptional enough to justify its telling. We tale-tellers are all Ancient Mariners, and none of us is warranted in stopping Wedding Guests (in other words, the hurrying public) unless he has something more unusual to relate than the ordinary experience of every average man and woman. The whole secret of fiction and the drama—in the constructional part—lies in the adjustment of things unusual to things eternal and universal. The writer who knows exactly how exceptional, and how non-exceptional, his events should be made, possesses the key to the art.

(Thomas Hardy, quoted by Miriam Allott, *Novelists On The Novel*, p. 58)

Everyone recognises that—whatever you call it—sexual love is for most people the most interesting and memorable aspect of life.

(John Bayley, *The Characters of Love*, p. 4)

What can compare with human sexuality in providing material for the novelist? This relation is both intrinsically and extrinsically fascinating, constituting as it does a series of interlocking para-doxes. It is at once an instinctual reflex carrying a humiliating reminder of our animal origins, and a primary means of express-ing the highest spiritual impulse known to man, the love of a fellow creature. Alexander the Great described sex as the insistent recollection of our mortality; yet the poets, who cannot lie, tell us again and again down the centuries what it is to be made immortal with a kiss. Sex travels so closely with love, that many participants assume or mistake the one to mean the other; it masquerades delusively as love, often claims to be or to serve in place of love; but life and literature alike abound in versions of that sexual experience which leaves the partners in the roles of murderer and victim. Who is not, however dimly, haunted by a wraith of some such past encounter? For some, this aberration becomes the norm, and the promised closeness which sexual activity implies reveals itself to be a dreary repetitive act of apartness:

> It was not so bad, she thought, when it was all over: not as bad as *that*. It meant nothing to her, nothing at all. Expecting outrage and imposition, she was relieved to find she felt nothing. She was able maternally to bestow the gift of herself on this humble stranger, and remain untouched. Women have an extraordinary ability to withdraw from the sexual relationship, to immunise themselves against it, in such a way that their men can be left feeling let down and insulted without having anything tangible to complain of.
>
> (Doris Lessing, *The Grass Is Singing*, 1950, p. 66)

The desolation suggested here, through the telling use of verbal echoes ("not so bad . . . not as bad . . . nothing . . . nothing . . . nothing . . .") is not the worst that can be experienced in this area of human behaviour; on the contrary it is in some ways the best that anyone in this situation can hope for, so easily does this most satisfactory become the least satisfactory of human contacts.

But sex activity is more than a perennially interesting theme. It is a touchstone of sexual attitudes, demanding as it does the willing cooperation of those whose culturation and conditioning have rendered them wary of if not hostile towards each other. Each sex is perpetually enforced to cope with received impressions and dictated concepts of responses appropriate both to their own and to the other sector; the relevant stereotypes alternately welcome and warn, beckon and threaten. Surely, then, if the difference between female and male writers is to be found anywhere, we should expect it to be manifested in the treatment of sex itself.

But are there any specifically male or female thematic approaches to what is, by definition, a mutual activity? One topic which has received attention from some of this century's most distinguished women writers has been the sex war. It is the continued implication of much of Ivy Compton-Burnett's fiction that each sex is capable of almost all aspects of the behaviour of the other; sexual stereotypes are usually the first (and last) resort of the scoundrel, susceptible to unimaginable permutations and manipulations, and hence to be regarded mainly as battle stations, as it were, in the sex war, rather than as tokens of any kind of "reality". The struggles for dominance for which her novels are famous are invariably sexual in nature; her potent females are those whose drives have been perverted and redirected into masculine forms in a world where female drive as such is not sanctioned, or at the least has not yet found a socially acceptable form. Happy marriages, simple contented liaisons, are unknown in the Compton-Burnett universe, so stark, so unblinking, so Swiftian even, is her assessment of the gaping discrepancy between form and content in human relationships. Those who believe that they love, or are loved, are frequently exposed as being hideously deceived and self-deceived. This devastating, almost intolerable cynicism, makes her among the most radical of writers on the theme of sex situations in society, although, relishing the irony, she enjoyed a reputation as a Jane Austenish old thing writing quaintly and wittily of the days of yesteryear. Her method of undermining received notions of behaviour, and of illustrating the embattled nature of sexual relations, is to show the machinery of sexual convention in its full traditional motion, and then to startle us with the logical and usually appalling outcome.

A typical example of this method is Sophia Stace in *Brothers And Sisters* (1950). This female tyrant, who later comes to occupy every nook and cranny of the novel she inhabits, is in the beginning slipped almost surreptitiously into our view as an unremarkable model of conventional daughterhood. The author's first concern is with the father who has shaped Sophia's ideas and manners:

> Andrew Stace was accustomed to say, that no man had ever despised him, and no man had ever broken him in. The omission of woman from his statement was due to his omission of her from his conception of executive life.

(p. 1)

It is precisely this that the book sets out to rectify. We are shown how Sophia is educated in tyranny and routine bullying by the daily behaviour of her father; we see, too, how the fact that she is female gives her an early grounding in devious methods of obtaining the results which her father achieves by head-on collision —"she took the method of gaining his esteem, of suppression of her character, and assumption of a sprightliness not her own" (pp. 5–6). Later in her life, trembling like so many of Ivy Compton-Burnett's characters on the edge of a terrible paranoia, Sophia is to exact from her own family every penny of the tribute she has been forced to pay to her father's blind egotism and rigidly structured concepts. Her whole life is directed towards answering and negating her father's decision to leave the family house to his adopted son rather than to her:

> Moreton Edge is not for a woman. The girl will have what will keep her in comfort if she doesn't marry, and make her husband respect her if she does. What more does a woman want? What more can she do with for herself or her family? What is the use of making a woman not a woman? I have never seen it work.

(p. 8)

The ensuing revelation that Christian is Andrew's illegitimate as well as adopted son does little to mitigate the offence from Sophia's point of view; nor does it disturb her conviction that she was right to marry the man who proves to be her half-brother, so overwhelming is the compulsion to outwit man the enemy by gaining and retaining Moreton Edge.

In any war, of course, it is a cardinal principle never to trust the enemy. Even when male characters appear to praise, understand, or defend women, they do so most characteristically from motives of self-seeking. Thus Duncan Edgeworth, the almost sadistically insensitive and pompous father of *A House And Its Head* (1935): "Why should a woman's youth be spotless, any more than a man's?" (p. 244). But this unexpected upsurge of feminism has to be taken in the overall context of his repeatedly expressed contempt for "old maids" and "brats"; moreover he says it to exculpate himself from certain peccadilloes and in addition to get his favourite daughter Sybil out of a scrape. This girl's name, with its echo of Disraeli's "Two Nations" and its

95

foreboding implications of witchcraft and preternatural capacity, later takes on a grim relevance as she reveals herself to be accomplished in lying, scheming, and, eventually, child murder. It is entirely in keeping with the hidden recesses of Duncan's nature that she is his preferred child. Further, his treatment of his first wife in her last illness, his refusal to allow the dying woman to remain in bed and so miss the family breakfast, his failure to acknowledge even that she is ill until she has slipped beyond his grasp, all evoke with bitter poignancy the thousand nameless cruelties of traditional masculine government.

Nowhere does Ivy Compton-Burnett hold out any hope of change or improvement in men's attitudes or women's consequent situations. The bland bullying Miles Mowbray (note the parody of long-standing English autocracy through the use of the family name of the Dukes of Norfolk) speaks for many generations, kinds, and degrees of men in the following:

> Of course women are not equal to men. They are not so strong or intelligent. That is, they have their own kind of intelligence. And a more important kind, of course. But they are not the same. Naturally they are different. Yes, you may laugh, Ellen. I know you think you are cleverer than I am. And you may be, for all I can say. Of course you are. We all recognise it. And if there is anyone who does so, it is your husband.

> (*A Father And His Fate*, p. 11)

The ultimate accolade, the masculine seal of approval. There are times when Ivy Compton-Burnett almost convinces us that the race of men deserve every drop of the shrivelling caustic irony she pours on them.

"The man, the male, the important person, the only person who matters." This phrase, from 1928, might have been taken straight from the pages of any of the new feminist publications of the nineteen-sixties and seventies. Readers who complain of the "stridency" of modern women writers might reflect upon the length of time during which women have been stating their case to an overwhelming silence from an apparently deaf world. Jean Rhys is, throughout her fiction, to be found making weary but still spirited gestures in the direction of the opposite sex; but with a subtler and tenderer gift than Ivy Compton-Burnett's, she constantly directs our attention towards the casualties in the sex war. All her work is illuminated by what Ford Madox Ford, in his preface to her first volume of short stories, *Left Bank* (1927), called her "terrific . . . almost lurid!—passion for stating the case of the underdog". Ford saw this as part of Jean Rhys's sympathy with the "left bank" of life itself, the sinister, the frightening, the out of order. Most of Jean Rhys's characters live among "the fools and the defeated", on that shabby fringe of society where the need for money, for release, for some assertion of the self as a necessity to survival, leads to financial and social offences and hence into conflict with the organised sections of the community. These offences are not presented as morally culpable; the money difficulties in "Vienne", the drunk and disorderly outbursts of the young West Indian girl in "Let Them Call It Jazz", two key stories in *Left Bank*, are set down without comment as symptoms of moral, social, and personal debilitude, to be regarded as what we, so many years later, are still learning to call a cry for help.

But it is not always necessary to commit an act outrageous to the limited sensibilities of the bourgeoisie to find yourself in trouble, as Jean Rhys sees it. Hers is a world where it is an offence to be old, ugly, or stupid, so harsh are the operations of the established and administrative classes. "From A French Prison", in *Left Bank*, gives us an old man and a boy waiting in a queue of visitors. The prison itself, with its bored, preoccupied guards, serves as a microcosm of a society which is both indifferent and incomprehensible to its members. The old man is confused and apprehensive; he doesn't speak the language (always a significant metaphor for this writer, whose work concentrates on the dispossessed inhabitants of several major European cities, notably Paris and London). He fails to hand in his permit, and is deprived of it in tears and fear, unable to grasp what is happening. Even in this early study of impotence, later to prove a major concern in Jean Rhys's work, the rich use of metaphor and symbol, and the evocative choice of location, are remarkable and distinctive features.

In the main, though, it is women who suffer. Jean Rhys does not indict the social system in vague or general terms. She always highlights its malfunctioning through some specific insult to one person in particular, and that person usually female. Typically Jean Rhys sees woman as a creature both frail and robust. She is handicapped in the daily battle by the inferiority of her weapons and by her crippling inner sensitivity. Yet at the same time she is fortified by a determination to survive, and by a compulsion to show no outward sign of "softness", for she believes that to seem soft automatically provokes hardness in others. *Postures* (1928), recently republished as *Quartet* with a regrettable loss of the social and sexual innuendo in the original title, offers the prototype Rhys anti-heroine. Marya Zelli is a bewildered expatriate whose marriage to a foreigner has robbed her of her own sense of nationality without providing a new one. Her reluctant association, through his shady and unsuccessful dealings, with the world of petty crime, precipitates her initiation into the dreary round of money shortage, letters home, appeals to men, subsistence on coffee and croissants. The dingy hotel room and the insolence of the waiters are a continuous bitter mockery of better times.

Below the surface realism of the detail, there is a vein of expressionism in Jean Rhys's work which may help to explain the reverberation of her writing. For instance, the linking of Marya's life with crime is a grim symbol of her "offence" against society, her inability to fit in with the conventional, the acceptable and safe. The "punishment", deprivation of cash, food, and a place to live, is, with nightmarish circularity, a further continuation of the "crime". In the course of things the experience of rejection becomes internalised; in the work of Jean Rhys female self-distrust and despair finds its extremist voice. All her heroines are run down by the lives they lead to the point of serious debility, almost illness. They can only endure each day by nursing themselves through it, like invalids. Here is Sasha, in *Good Morning Midnight* (1939), returning to Paris:

> I have been here five days. I have decided on a place to eat in at midday, a place to eat in at night, a place to have my drink in after dinner. I have arranged my little life.

This stress on the "realities" of life serves to highlight the narrator's acquaintance with the terrible underworld, the subculture inhabited by those without income, security, function (this, of course, very characteristic of middle-class writing in the Depression era). There is a dreamlike quality to much of the prose here, with a consistent use of dislocation techniques; the heroine looks into a mirror and sees through it the movement of her past, as in the moment of drowning. In this treatment of the sensations of the excluded, the progress through perplexity to panic, the exhausting emotional oscillation between the frenetic and the torpid, Jean Rhys is often reminiscent of Kafka. Like Kafka's K, the Rhys heroine is broken on the wheel of repeated hopeless attempts to placate the implacable, the impenetrable and inexorable machine of authority. There is, too, something Kafkaesque about Jean Rhys's irony, her feeling that the whole of life is just one long unspeakable practical joke. A characteristic moment occurs when one of Marya's complacent acquaintances advises her that she should try to "retrieve" her damaged fortunes by becoming a *"femme nue"* in a nightclub.

As this "joke" suggests, the work of Jean Rhys has certain affinities with that of Camus. But for her the Outsider is always female. It is her recurrent, almost obsessive theme, that women are permanent and perpetual victims of masculine society. Not only will they be oppressed by individual male bullies; they are everywhere confronted by institutionalised masculine hostility in the shape of the law, the professions, the police, the bureaucrats, of every country. Jean Rhys is thus one of few women writers to make explicit the link between the sex war and the class struggle. To be female is to inhabit, without hope of escape, the lowest class of all in a sexist structure. Men may work, singly or in units, either to improve their own position on the social scale, or to revolutionise a situation which makes dealing in these terms inevitable. Women, denied any such recourse, flit about on the edges of the "real" world, dependent on men for maintaining even the most unsatisfactory of existences within it.

One of her most deeply-felt attacks on the system is couched in the form of a mental monologue by Sasha, who has just been humiliated and dismissed by her employer. Note how the economic factor in female dependence is brought out, as well as the enfeeblement of the victim of such treatment:

> Well, let's argue this out, Mr Blank. You, who represent Society, have the right to pay me four hundred francs a month. That's my market value, for I am an inefficient member of Society, slow on the

uptake, uncertain, slightly damaged in the fray, there's no denying it. So you have the right to pay me four hundred francs a month, to lodge me in a small, dark room, to clothe me shabbily, to harass me with worry and monotony and unsatisfied longings till you get me to the point when I blush at a look, cry at a word. We can't all be happy, we can't all be rich, we can't all be lucky— and it would all be so much less fun if we were. Isn't that so, Mr Blank? There must be the dark background to show up the bright colours. Some must cry so that others may be able to laugh the more heartily. Sacrifices are necessary. . . . Let's say you have this mystical right to cut my legs off. But the right to ridicule me afterwards because I am a cripple—no, that I think you haven't got. And that's the right you hold most dearly, isn't it? You must be able to despise the people you exploit. But I wish you a lot of trouble, Mr Blank, and just to start off with, your damned shop's going bust. Alleluia! Did I say all this? Of course I didn't. I didn't even think it.

(*Good Morning Midnight*, p. 29)

Sasha speaks here for all the exploited, all the underpaid and helpless. But it is Jean Rhys's talent to be able to alter the focus from the general to the particular at will, and usually to significant effect. Her presentation of Sasha is also managed through some painful images of specifically female despair, crying in the *lavabo* under the gaze of the attendant, or feeling, at best, "Saved, rescued, fished-up, half-drowned, out of the deep, dark river, dry clothes, hair shampooed and set" (p. 10). And few women writers have so skilfully summoned up the accelerating anxieties and needs of the female growing older: "Now, money, for the night is coming. Money for my hair, money for my teeth, money for shoes that won't deform my feet (It's not easy now to walk around in cheap shoes with very high heels), money for good clothes, money, money. The night is coming" (p. 144). In Sasha's consciousness, her "film-mind" as she calls it, males play varying but always hurtful parts. At one stage she is tormented by a whore's dream of an *apache*:

I am in a little whitewashed room. The sun is hot outside. A man is standing with his back to me . . . I am wearing a black dress, very short, and heelless slippers. My legs are bare. I am watching for the expression on the man's face when he turns round. Now he ill-treats me, now he betrays me. He often brings home other women and I have to wait on them, and I don't like that. But as long as he is alive and near me I am not unhappy. If he were to die I should kill myself.

Later she is shaken by a harsh blast of self-disgust and caricatures herself viciously as aged and sexually pretentious: "What an amusing ten days! Positively packed with thrills. The last performance of What's-her-name And Her Boys or It Was All Due To An Old Fur Coat. Positively the last performance. . . ." The irony in the last phrase is made clear in the novel's stunning climax in which the man who offers sex offers also death and in full awareness Sasha embraces the two experiences, which have for her always been one.

After the appearance of *Good Morning Midnight* in 1939, Jean Rhys ceased publishing for many years. Her recent emergence from this self-imposed silence shows that her major preoccupations have developed, but not changed. Womanhood remains, to her, a nightmare dystopia, since a deep fear and hatred motivate the behaviour of men towards women. Male seeks female as his natural adversary; sex *is* war. In the context of this theme, the wartime setting provides more than a historical backdrop to "I Spy A Stranger" (*Penguin Modern Stories 1*, 1969, pp. 53–67); it acts as a continuing image of the relations between the sexes, where polarisation determines opposing roles and makes impossible any sort of civilised or humane living. Male aggression reduces the female by stages to foreigner, enemy, refugee; she may resist, but she cannot win.

The victim in this case is Laura, who because of the fighting in Europe has been forced to give up her life there and return to England to lodge with a married cousin for the duration. Here she arouses the hostility of the cousin's husband, who persecutes her and finally drives her into a geriatric asylum. Laura is thus the victim of male belligerence twice over; she loses home, friends, lover, through the external conflict, and refuge, sanity, freedom through her defeat on the domestic front; and Jean Rhys makes it plain which of the two she considers to be the real war. Such is the nature of the sex war, Jean Rhys implies, that certain women need do nothing in order to draw male fire. They provoke simply by what they are. Laura never offers any insult to the husband. But she challenges him indirectly by displaying in aggregate many

101

characteristics which are traditionally if unconsciously felt as offences in a female; she is single, she is "brainy", and she is old. Because she has lived abroad she is regarded as suspiciously un-English—these two features are united in the abusive village nickname for her, "the witch of Prague". Further, she is by temperament reclusive and literary, and her actions and preferences in this respect are subtly used to increase her isolation and to stress its pathos. We see her writing endless letters, keeping a diary, cutting out newspaper reports and sticking them into a scrapbook. As in Doris Lessing's *The Golden Notebook* where the heroine does the same thing as her breakdown gathers momentum, this activity is seen as an apt evocation of the fragmentation of her life, its final resolution into the sensational and ephemeral.

All this is the work of men, the enemy. At times we seem to be in an inverse Strindbergian landscape, and Jean Rhys insists on her interpretation with a rather rigid contrivance by which none of the male characters is permitted any warmth, gentleness, or even common human decency (this recalls Strindberg's treatment of the female characters in, say, *The Father, The Dance Of Death,* and *The Stronger*). The husband, Ricky, as his name suggests, is conceived of in the diminutive, the perennial schoolboy, emotionally retarded at the stage of truculence towards and inability to cope with the female sex. Male humour is the first weapon with which Ricky seeks to prove and to place Laura. Jean Rhys's bitter assessment of the reality of intersex warfare emerges nowhere so clearly as in this sequence, where Ricky is vulgarly cruel under the mask of geniality and goodwill. Annoyed by Laura's attempts to obtain news of her friends in occupied Europe, Ricky decides to "laugh her out of it". He offers as a joke the idea of "the Gestapo getting her sweetheart". Her reaction to this confirms him in his view that "the old girl's got no sense of humour at all". Part of the joke for Ricky lies in the thought of an "old girl" having a "sweetheart", though we are told that Laura has; this is an important theme in Jean Rhys, the continuance of love among those whom orthodox society feels are, or rightly should be, beyond it.

At last verbal persecution gives way to the physical violence which it has for some time been hiding. Becoming increasingly paranoid about Laura, Ricky details his wife to tell her that she must go (a shrewd glance, this, at both his cowardice and his immaturity in the retreat behind the female). As she is leaving, Ricky decides to speed the parting guest. Approaching her with one of his crass jokes—"It's moving day"—he takes her arm to hurry her downstairs. At his touch she breaks down, screaming and swearing. She clings to the bannisters, and Ricky attacks her, hitting and kicking, and drags her downstairs. Beaten, dazed, and more than half mad, she is whirled away in a taxi. But even in the grim asylum of his choice Laura is not safe from Ricky's malice—he announces that she can only stay there as long as her own money lasts—and the reader is left to speculate upon a future which Jean Rhys has managed so that it presents not a spark of hope.

All the other men in the story are introduced to reinforce the effect of male brutality. A friend of Ricky, one Fluting (the name indicates the author's derisive view of his capacities) is used to illustrate Jean Rhys's concept of that area of the masculine mentality in which sexual and military matters unite with a peculiarly indecent flourish. This is principally brought out through the symbolism of weapons—obscene letters threaten "A Gun for the Old Girls", and the old cliché is given a new significance in the remark of his wife that Ricky has "got his knife into Laura". Fluting is an underwear man. He tells Laura that "the Waafs up at the station smelt", and waxes "sarcastic about their laundry allowance". In the general context of this piece, Laura's vigorous counter-attack—"Sir, they smell; you stink"—seems not a victory but a defeat, a descent to Fluting's level. Further, the direct echo of one of Dr Johnson's most famous remarks highlights Laura's pathos and frailty by the evocation of this vigorous and articulate old man.

And males band together, Jean Rhys warns. The crisis for Laura comes, symbolically, at the height of the worst air-raid of the war, when her neglect of her blackout curtain unites against her the forces of law and order in the forms of the air-raid warden and the police. The police are doubly enemies, of sex and class, as males and as custodians of the male social order. They have "a good laugh" (male humour again) over Laura's diary-scrapbook, and Ricky gives orders that it must be destroyed. Even the doctor, who might be thought impartial, comes to Laura not in his office

103

of healer but because Ricky sends for him in order to get Laura certified. The doctor refuses this, but out of professional cussedness, not true sympathy. The level of his concern for his patient is shown in the following exchange:

> Pratt asked her if she was willing to go to a sanatorium for a rest and she said "Why not?" Ricky shouted at her "You get off to your sanatorium pronto. You ought to have been there long ago." "You're being inhuman," Pratt said. Ricky said, "Well, will the bloody old fool keep quiet?" Pratt told him he'd guarantee that.

Set against this efficient male bonding, even between men who are antipathetic to each other, like Ricky and Pratt, is the inability of women to offer even the most elementary support for one another. Laura's cousin, Mrs. Hudson, cannot help her, though aware of her sufferings. This woman is implicated in Laura's story not only through the narrative connection, but structurally, by Jean Rhys's use of a framing device by which Mrs Hudson relates the events to her sister, Mrs Trant. A key passage makes clear the interaction of all the women's lives. The diary writing, the only part of Laura that we encounter directly, is used to convey her sense of the reduction of life and the erosion of her personality. She feels "like a cog in a machine"; she sees herself as "shamming dead". But above all she is alienated, literally, by the English attitude to women. This piece involves the sisters in Laura's plight, drawing added importance from the fact that Laura's voice is reaching us from the grave of the asylum, and through the mist of the incomprehension of the two women who are reading it together:

> There is something strange about the attitude to women as women. Not the dislike (or fear). That isn't strange of course. But it's all so completely taken for granted, and surely that is strange. It has settled down and become an atmosphere, or, if you like, a climate, and no one questions it, least of all the women themselves. There is *no* opposition. The effects are criticized, for some of the effects are hardly advertisements for the system, the cause is seldom mentioned, and then very gingerly. The few mild ambiguous protests usually come from men. Most of the women seem to be carefully trained to revenge any unhappiness that they feel on each other, or on children—or on any individual man who

happens to be at a disadvantage. In dealing with men as a whole, a streak of subservience, of servility, usually appears, something cold, calculating, lacking in imagination.

But no one can go against the spirit of a country with impunity and propaganda from the cradle to the grave can do a lot.

This thematic statement stands at the centre of the story. It has been prepared for by the account of Laura as outsider and victim, and as such describes her condition; the second part of the story illustrates its general truth by showing how accurately it sums up the other women's situation. They too have regarded Laura as an enemy because of her refusal to accept the social order accepted by them (that of male dominance). But they have enough of her in them, in every sense, to feel her misery. Their failure to help her is seen as a failure of sex loyalty as well as of blood, for both turn against her mainly under pressure from their husbands. So Laura's thoughts are deeply relevant to them, and they are glimmeringly alive to this. Mrs Hudson has "moments" when she agrees with Laura. Mrs Trant finds it "nonsense", but her thoughts turn anxiously to her favourite daughter, who not only liked Laura, but opposed her father in standing up for her. Mrs Trant had taken the slave's covert delight in any defiance of the master, but now feels that it was bad: "A girl ought to play safe, ought to go with the tide, it was a bad sign when a girl liked unpopular people." The duty of young females to make themselves acceptable overcomes her. She fearfully imagines Judy growing up to be unhappy (another Laura, perhaps) and considers her sister a "sterile old fool" for offering the view that Judy is "tough". This further extension of the web of hostility between women is not only Jean Rhys's way of supporting and developing Laura's pronouncement. It also explains why they cannot unite against the enemy in mutual help.

A final touch neatly catches up this aspect of the theme. The "home", says Mrs Hudson, where Laura has gone, has a golf links for the patients. " 'But does she play golf?' said Mrs Trant. 'Let's hope,' said Mrs Hudson, 'let's hope'. . . ." The sentimentalist may find in that a comforting reassurance of the unfailing warm concern of the gentler sex for one another. It seems more likely, however, that it is intended to emphasise not only the hopelessness of Laura's fate, but also the dismal prospect for the women who "survive". Hope is all they have. It is standard currency among the hopeless. Jean Rhys invites us all to appreciate the joke.

In this suggestion that there is no real possibility of individual freedom for women, since they are moulded from their earliest years into conventionally acceptable forms, Jean Rhys touches a nerve which has caused many women writers to wince, both in the nineteenth and twentieth centuries. A rather more light-hearted study of the process is to be found in Iris Murdoch's Annette, the younger of the heroines of *The Flight From The Enchanter* (1956). Of all Iris Murdoch's novels to date, this one is the most explicitly "about" the sex war, and interest has mainly centred on the lurid tale of Rosa and her twin Draculae, the Polish brothers, not to mention the dotty ancient suffragettes and the complementary masculine machinations of Mischa Fox and Calvin Blick. But the part played by Annette is a substantial contribution to the theme of woman's imprisonment in conventional roles. In a novel where the other women characters are successively essaying politics, work, mothering, mantrapping, and self-beautification in their search for fulfilled womanhood, and where they all, moreover, stand measured against the long shadow of Rosa Luxemburg, Annette is the perpetual girl-child.

She is first introduced to us in connection with her expensive finishing school, which draws attention to her unfinished childhood, her little-girl name, her habit of running and skipping, and her juvenile vocabulary ("beastly", "horrid"). Even her fairly systematic acquisition of clothes and jewels is not the mark of a mature female, but a pathetic reminder of her unvalued and unsatisfactory childhood, and an attempt to stabilise her environment at a pleasant level. Despite a gush of sentimental pity for "the poor Minotaur" when she encounters his story, Annette is blind to the real implications of this dark and ancient tale, as she is also to the feelings of those around her. Not only is she in the grip of the narcissism of adolescence; the fish and mermaid imagery with which she is associated convey her cold, half-developed intersex quality. This is reinforced by the fact that she is half of yet another of Iris Murdoch's terrible twins, and as a result, through her close love for and dependence on her brother, only half a person.

But Annette is also a nubile young woman and it is in her efforts to define herself in this respect that she runs into trouble. There is about her a strong suggestion of the capricious princess of fairy-tales; we are told that for her the "essence of freedom" lies in the notion that people are ceaselessly toiling for her benefit. When Annette is surprised at the dressmaker's by the novel's central character and source of power, Mischa Fox, Nina the dressmaker removes the half-made dress from her, leaving her in her underwear before him as if she were a child or a dummy. It is not made clear whether Nina is motivated in her attempt to neutralise Annette as a sexual presence by jealousy or by a wish to protect the younger woman from this latter-day Volpone. Either way, Annette is not to be put off from spreading her wings. She counters Nina's move by making a bold but essentially schoolgirl pass at Mischa—"Will you take me in your car to my next appointment?"—the last phrase being, of course, like the sea-green brocade dress for which she is being fitted, an attempt to evoke or simulate the aura of the sophisticated worldly woman. Later, in a more down-to-earth sexual situation with Rainborough, she wavers between the adolescent, warily scenting out possible adult irony, and the female entirely at ease with the trite and time-dishonoured conventions of womanhood: " 'I don't know,' said Annette, 'I'm not much good at anything.' She smiled in a helpless feminine way."

As the situation develops along traditional lines, Annette's poise increases. Rainborough's laboured and inexpert grope brings out her superficial expertise, and she is quite in command, even ironic at his expense—"I'm afraid I can't recall your Christian name," she says as he attempts to insert his hand into her blouse. What she values, however, as Iris Murdoch makes quite clear, is the conventional structure of what is evidently for her a highly conventional occasion. She submits, "doll-like", with the traditional token opposition—"John, please!"—as he exposes her breasts. But she is not yet woman enough to take any responsibility for the mutuality of the experience. What enrages her, and causes her to resist his further advances, is his pompous insistence that she is "making this scene" as much as he is. Unable to tolerate this crude breaking of the convention, Annette unexpectedly reverts to type, becomes "a powerful fish" in his grasp, cold, sinewy, all eyes. But this upsurge of her mermaid self exhausts her, and when an unexpected visitor arrives to disturb the amorous proceedings, she submits, doll-like again, to Rainborough's panic, and is thrust unresistingly into the china cupboard (is there an echo of the famous "china" scene in *The Country Wife* here?). Passive, submissive, she remains there throughout a long colloquy between Rainborough and his visitor, and even then, recovered half-naked and half-dead from the cupboard, weeping and crushed, she still feels the primitive female compulsion to exonerate the male and shoulder the blame: "It wasn't your fault, John." But John, not surprisingly, has gone off the boil, and feels nothing for Annette so strongly as an intense weariness and a desire for her departure.

None of Iris Murdoch's riddling morals is easily drawn from the gorgeously lush and fleshy symbolism of her imaginative landscape. But this seems to be one of her plainer lessons for ladies, that the careful cultivation of the appropriate role mannerisms may well be just a waste of time. Men are not really drawn or moved by what has been so effortfully acquired and produced. Annette is linked in this with the well-groomed Harpies of Rainborough's civil service section. Many critics have commented on the prevalence in Iris Murdoch's work of long abundant hair as a symbol of natural vitality,[1] and the Harpies are caricatured through their artificial and unnaturally set hair which they adopt in compliance with prevailing beauty conventions.

Paradoxically, not only are these "beauty" devices inefficacious, but they also serve to activate the antifeminist feelings latent in the hearts of many men, and not a few women too. It seems that criticism has not so far sufficiently considered the ways in which moral, aesthetic, and intellectual distaste for women are mingled in many fictional presentations. This is, naturally, relevant only to those situations in which women attract attention or break into the "real world". All too often they are insignificant to the point of invisibility, and Carson McCullers, among others, has written

[1] For an interesting discussion of both James's and Ibsen's use of this image, as well as all other aspects of the connections between the novelist and the playwright, see Michael Egan's *Henry James: The Ibsen Years* (1972).

persuasively on this theme in *The Heart Is A Lonely Hunter* (1943), pp. 270–1:

> "This here is a riddle," George said.
> "I listening."
> "Two Indians was walking on a trail. The one in front was the son of the one behind, but the one behind was not his father. What kin was they?"
> "Less see. His stepfather."
> George grinned at Portia with his little square, blue teeth.
> "His uncle, then."
> "You can't guess. It was his mother. The trick is that you don't think about an Indian being a lady."

There is a further irony here, in that this is young George Kelly, son of a poor white Irish immigrant family, talking to the negro servant, Portia; in this one suggestive moment Carson McCullers incorporates all the downgraded and struggling, thus linking the oppression of women with racism in the structure of society. Clearly you don't have to be female to be undervalued and over-worked, and to be treated like a knot in the woodwork by family and friends; but it sometimes helps.

Fortunate however is the female character in fiction who can escape that reflex antifeminism in sex characterisation which strongly suggests that SS. Paul and Augustine ride again. We have so far only considered the comments of selected women writers on the sex war in the twentieth-century novel. Now, in the red corner, I give you the men. The diarist Aubrey may have believed that " 'tis not consistent with an harmonical soul to be a woman-hater", but a great deal of the characterisation of women recalls Lord Chesterfield's remark to his son that women are "only children of larger growth"; and the attitude of some male authors would lead one to suppose that they must have been bitten by women in their infancy. Fictional representation of antifeminism has been a staple of literature from its origins, often by men who must at the least be accounted as sympathetic to the cause of women. It was an old tale that Chaucer gave his pilgrims through the mouth of the Wife of Bath, and Shakes-peare similarly must have rekindled many an ancient grudge in the words of Posthumus:

For there's no motion
That tends to vice in man but I affirm
It is the woman's part; be it lying, note it
The woman's; flattering, hers; deceiving, hers;
Lust and rank thoughts, hers, hers; revenges, hers;
Ambitions, covetings, changes of pride, disdain,
Nice longings, slanders, mutability,
All faults that man may name, nay, that Hell knows,
Why hers, in part, or all; but rather, all;
For even to vice
They are not constant, but are changing still
One vice but of a minute old for one
Not half so old as that. I'll write against them,
Detest them, curse them.

(Cymbeline, II. v. 20–33)

Posthumus abandoned his purpose upon the reconciliation with Imogen, whose imagined faithlessness provoked this outburst. But his cause is not forgotten. Katharine Rogers has made a study of antifeminism in literature, *The Troublesome Helpmate: A History of Misogyny in Literature* (1966). It is interesting to note in passing how many books by women writers on woman writers use, half ironically and half apologetically, the derogatory comments of antifeminists upon their sex—*Frail Vessels, Their Proper Sphere, The Singular Anomaly*, and *The Troublesome Helpmate*, are all labels which would be best left unresurrected, even in irony. Katharine Rogers inevitably devotes considerable attention to D. H. Lawrence in a fine section which need not be parroted here. What does appear plainly from her treatment is the fact that not all antifeminism takes its source from the sort of grotesque hostility of Posthumus, which Shakespeare presents firmly as a temporary breakdown, an obscene derangement like the sexual jealousy of Othello and Leontes. There is an implicit and inescapable antifeminism in any insistence upon the difference between the sexes.

For Captain Harville, in *Persuasion* (Chapter XXIII) is by no means the only man to believe sincerely on behalf of his sex that there exists "a true analogy between our bodily frames and our mental; and that as our bodies are the strongest, so are our feelings; capable of bearing most rough usage, and riding out the heaviest weather". Comparisons are odorous, said Dogberry; but they will continue to be made. C. B. Cox, in *The Free Spirit* (1963), p. 1, has drawn attention to the importance of the cult of bullhood in the modern novel, with reference to its disparaging implications: "that educated liberals lack vitality has been a repeated theme in many novels of the last hundred years". He comments on the fictional use of women characters to restore the men's faith in life and in themselves. But how much more are women derogated and disvalued by the masculine way of life and standard of values, and who is to restore *their* faith? Think of the advice of Captain MacWhirr in Conrad's *Typhoon* (1903): "Facing it—always facing it—that's the way to get through. You are a young sailor. Face it. That's enough for any man" (Chapter V). The implicit assumption here is that strength and endurance, and learning the skill of these qualities, are inherently masculine and required only by males because of the nature of their different lives and work.

It seems likely (and hopeful) that this ideal of heroic self-fulfilment is being eroded by increasing knowledge of psychology and mounting uncertainty about the needs and entitlements of the white Anglo-Saxon Protestant male. Today's hero is more likely to be found dodging it than facing it—be it work, conformity, the draft, or the girl next door. But one at least of our most celebrated twentieth-century men writers spent a great deal of time and energy in his life contriving it. Where danger, the enemy, the man's life with the sun at your back and the gun in your hand, did not exist, Ernest Hemingway continuously and quite literally went hunting for them, or made them up. This fact may explain the dangerous absurdity of much of Hemingway's fiction. The MacWhirr stance, relevant both in style and matter to a genuinely extreme situation, becomes ridiculous when the occasion is sought, created, even manufactured, as in Hemingway. The He-man Hem-hero appears too clearly as the fictional projection of the wished self. Poor Hem! and with what a slight shift of focus does big man turn into little boy. The famous preference for primitive over Anglo-Saxon women, the weakness for little pussy girls, furry and feline, the conviction that mothers are failures, that if women are not subjugated they can only be destructive, and that the truly virile man does without them, chooses trout-fishing instead, all suggest a temperament marked

111

by fear and inability to cope rather than that of the modern Tarzan of his admirers' apprehension. What else is the reader to make of the short story "Now I lay me . . ." in *Men Without Women* (1927), *The Sun Also Rises* (1926), or *Across The River And Into The Trees* (1950)?

But the stress is always on the heroic compulsion, and Hemingway was not writing for anyone likely to be reading Freud between the lines. Indeed, in his rejection of the twentieth century, in his search for a purer, cleaner time of heroes, Hemingway was trying to discover some escape from ideas so disruptive of a man's peace of mind as Freud's. And in the Hemingway world, where value lies in action, and the highest form of reflection is response, where the very shaping performance of the intellect is deliberately suspended as an expression of weakness, the feminine will automatically have little place. There is not time for meditation, for tenderness, for the exercise of the gentler emotions, when the chips are down, the numbers up, and the clichés whistling like hailstones about our ears. What is interesting about Hemingway's attitude is that he has precious little time for women anyway. At best they provide a restful interlude, and the opportunity for what another great hero, Lord Montgomery, termed "horizontal refreshment".

For like Lawrence, Hemingway basically apprehended women as functions or stages in a man's life, rather than as autonomous individuals. He too felt convinced that at the difficult and demanding moments of life, a man has to go it alone; women simply are not capable of following. The total androcentricity of Hemingway's thought is well illustrated in *The Snows of Kilimanjaro*; here the dying big-game hunter and writer (recognise anybody from the description?) drinks deep of the spring of terminal philosophy and comes up with "Love is a dunghill . . . and I'm the cock that gets on to it to crow". The best of his conclusions about his wife, who lovingly tends him, can only be categorised as condescending: "Why should he blame this woman because she kept him well?" Why indeed? But this is the kindest impulse that he feels for her, and she is shown not only as ineffectual but as excluded by her impercipience even from the knowledge that her husband is in fact dying.

But simple density is not the only reproach Hemingway offers to womankind. He had in fact a far greater fear than that of being misunderstood. Through his nightmares stalked a totally ruthless and destructive female, and much of his writing may be construed as an effort to exorcise her. It is indicative of this feeling that women appear high on Hemingway's list of what destroys writers, above drink, money, ambition, and other evils. (See, on this point, Mark Schorer, *The World We Imagine*, 1969, p. 377.) Occasionally this trait is associated with aristocratic women (again cf. Lawrence) like Lady Brett Ashley in *The Sun Also Rises*. More usually it is just plain female. A classic picture of the female predator is the wife of the eponymous hero of *The Short Happy Life Of Francis Macomber*; she can only tolerate her husband as the moral equivalent of the seven-stone weakling, and shoots him down as he finds his courage by killing a buffalo; when he "grows up", in Hemingway terms, that is, stops being afraid of big game. With complete disregard for consistency of characterisation, Hemingway then pushes on to make the wife pay for it. He feels he cannot leave the memory of Macomber without having the other member of the safari, the white hunter Wilson, somehow punish the destructive wife. But what can we think of a fearsome predatory bitch, more deadly than the animals of the jungle, who after the kill capitulates instantly before Wilson's reproof and collapses into feebly drivelling "Oh, please stop it. . . . Please, please stop it"? Here, as elsewhere, the need to reassure the threatened masculine ego and restore the *status quo* overrode aesthetic and artistic considerations. Always, always, the dreadful drive to create some consolation for his psychic injuries dulled his better judgment. Listen as he bluffs it out through the mouth of Harry Morgan, the dog-eared warrior-god of *To Have And To Have Not* (1937):

> The hell with my arm. You lose an arm you lose an arm. There's worse things than lose an arm. You've got two arms and you've got two of something else. And a man's still a man with one arm or with one of those.

(p. 98)

But these thoughts cannot keep out the cold. Among Harry's regrets in life is his failure to have a son, as he finds his three daughters "not much". His wife comforts him with the old wives' favourite ego-booster: "That's because you're such a man. That

113

way it always comes out girls." The portentous solemnity of this primitive mysogynistic nonsense would bring a smile to almost any lip, and not necessarily that of the feminist, but for an element of insistent pathos which at times is almost strong enough to overcome critical detachment. If ever a man unwittingly stripped his sleeve and showed his scars, it was Hemingway. The pomposity, the absurdity, only highlight our sense of the waste and pity of it all. The irresistible connection is with Pope's unexpectedly compassionate verdict on Addison in the *Epistle to Dr Arbuthnot*:

> Who but must laugh, if such a man there be?
> Who would not weep, if Atticus were he?

The tides of time have flowed fast in our century; too fast for Hemingway, who was at the last abandoned and washed up (in both senses of the term), a great beached whale contemplating with bitter distaste the antics of the minnows who were to survive him. It is hard not to share some of his feeling in contemplating the redefinition of the hero in recent fiction. We have no cause to be complacent about those novels of the last decade or so which seem to adopt or reflect a more modern standard of masculine behaviour. Their "trendiness" is superficial, and as undesirable and unpleasing as the noun which describes the attribute. The more free of hampering convention twentieth-century fictional characters become, the more freely they display their creators' deeply-cultured notions of male and female, their prejudices and resentments.

This thought should provide a sightline upon a particularly trying modern character-genre, that of the free, clever, sensitive, resourceful young man fending off a dim, grim suppressive female. She is presented as going by instinct through her ordained feminine task of narrowing horizons all round and dragging the thoughtful, cheerful, and sensitive down to her own level. He has to think for both of them, and twice as fast as one of them, for in his spirited and successful rebellion lies the hope for the future. The character is not new—the description would approximate to the heroes of H. G. Wells's *Love and Mr Lewisham* (1900) and *The History of Mr Polly* (1910)—but it is indicative of the temper of recent times that it is receiving such a thorough revival.

Historically its re-emergence is linked with the "angry young man" cult of the nineteen-fifties. The modern prototype in drama is John Osborne's Jimmy Porter. Another, more whimsical, example is *Billy Liar* by Keith Waterhouse and Willis Hall. But quite contemporaneously the novelists were evolving their own version, and deriving from another Jim, Kingsley Amis's lucky one, this tiresome fellow has wandered through the pages of John Wain, Stan Barstow, Alan Sillitoe, and is still going strong. Any female, no matter how good or bad, is primarily a landmark on the hero's road to self-definition, and must never be allowed to get ideas above this station. The bad ones, like Lucky Jim's Margaret, a man must nerve himself to leave behind as quickly as possible; the good ones are the prize at the end of the road. Joe, in John Braine's *Room At The Top* (1957) "learns", as "a truth", that the ownership of the attractive girl is "simply a question of money, of the price of the diamond ring on her left hand".

The characterisation of Joe, in all its crudity, plainly exhibits the trap of this fictional type, which Mary McCarthy has called "the pitiless phoney-detector" and has derived from the Hemingway hero. Where he is the custodian of all standards and values, and at the same time displays such a woeful impoverishment of principle, feeling, and even vocabulary, as Joe does, then there is no way of escaping the apparently unrelated pitfalls of his being both a boor and a prig. But it is already pitching it too high to consider the novel in this way. From its first pages the discerning reader will sum it up for what it is, a painfully earnest trip through the "Ah-Bisto!" land of young man's fancy. There is a diagrammatic simplicity in the presentation of the two goddesses of adolescent male fantasy, Mother-Earth Alice (the one with the big breasts) and Sweet Sue (the one with the rich daddy). The man who wakes from such a dream may, quite understandably, cry to dream again, and John Braine has become rich on the proceeds—but what does the woman dream, meanwhile?

Perhaps she dreams of the day when female characters in fiction are no longer so widely represented as points of development in men's growth and fulfilment, but as fully sentient and responsible beings. Perhaps her sights are lower, and she is merely hoping that in the fiction of the future she will break free of the domination of the disparaging generalisation—"Women adore to be noticed"; "Lawrence strove to put woman back in her rightful place"; "Women have no characters at all". And so on. These categorising and reductive statements may be picked out by the handful from the fiction of almost any time and place. They have been important, probably invaluable masculine weapons in the relationship of male and female which has been called the sex war. On the whole, in literature, the men have attacked, while the women have numbered their losses and counted their dead. There have been a few ineffective guerilla skirmishes from female territory, but no organised onslaught on the firmly-defended stronghold of masculine superiority. Although women writers have commented on the sex war, their writings are devoid of any sustained androgynistic tendencies, although much of the work of their male colleagues can be shown to be antifeminist through and through.

Perhaps the explanation of this lies in the female quality identified by Elaine Morgan in *The Descent of Woman* (1972), pp. 268–9, the refusal to lump all men together as the enemy:

> What we surely mustn't do is to try to found a women's movement on a kind of pseudo-male bonding, alleging the whole male sex to be a ferocious leopard, and whipping up hatred against it . . . . As a bonding mechanism it just won't work. Most women don't hallucinate that easily. You may raise the alarm and beat the drum, but when you point your finger at the enemy, most of them will say: "No, those aren't leopards. That's the postman, and that one is my son, and the one with the nice blue eyes is the one who was so kind to us last winter when there was all that snow." And they will be right.

If this is, as it seems, an accurate and down-to-earth assessment of female mental processes, then women have even greater grounds for objecting to being lumped together in their turn. Milton tells us that Adam and Eve lived "He for God only, she for God in him". Now, at last, after all these millennia, it is time for the process to be reversed. The onus is on all men, whether writers or not, to search for the spark of divine particularity which is every human birthright, in each individual woman.

5

Moral Themes and the Consolations of Romance

There was an innate refinement, a languid queenly *hauteur* about Gerty which was unmistakably evidenced in her delicate hands and higharched instep. Had kind fate but willed her to be born a gentlewoman of high degree in her own right and had she only received the benefit of a good education Gerty MacDowell might easily have held her own beside any lady in the land and have seen herself exquisitely gowned with jewels on her brow, patrician suitors at her feet vying with one another to pay their devoirs to her. Mayhap it was this, the love that might have been, that lent to her softly featured face at whiles a look, tense with suppressed meaning, that imparted a strange yearning tendency to the beautiful eyes a charm few could resist. Why have women such eyes of witchery?

(James Joyce, *Ulysses*, 1922, Penguin edition, p. 346)

Be good sweet maid, and let who can be clever;
Do lovely things, not dream them, all day long;
And so make Life, and Death, and that For Ever,
One grand sweet song.

(Charles Kingsley, *A Farewell to C.E.G.*)

The spirit of romance, both in its original and its debased forms, is a vitally influential element of contemporary fiction. As we have seen, masculine romance of the Hemingway type is implicit with antifeminism. The ideal and the reality of woman is assaulted by man's romanticisation of his own brutality and inadequacy, while any exaltation of the male usually involves as a matter of course the disvaluation of the female. This is not always achieved

117

simplistically through mockery or belittlement, nor is it always intended derogatorily by the author. On the contrary, the young soldier's love for Lyubov in Solzhenitsyn's *The Love-Girl And The Innocent* (1969) is an expression of spiritual aspiration and a proof that he has retained his humanity and is not yet dwindled into pure ravening ego like the rest of the camp inmates. But even in this context we are reminded that there is something deforming to the female in the male fantasisation of her into a complementary and, typically, a non-competitive figure. The soldier does not intend the offer of his love to be taken in this way, but the "love-girl" senses it as based on an imperfect acceptance of her nature, and is correspondingly uneasy.

Another kind of antifeminism, and one more deeply ingrained in the British novel tradition, is the requiring by male authors of their female characters that they suppress independence of mind, and freedom of body or soul, on pain of being presented as a freak. Dickens in particular stiffens his narratives with monitory cases of out-of-hand females. Consider the terrible trio in *Bleak House* (1853); Mrs Snagsby, the neurotic henpecker, held up as an example of wives who pay too much attention to their husband's, Mrs Jellyby and Mrs Pardiggle, glutinous images of wives who pay too little. It is axiomatic in Dickens that women who concern themselves with extra-domestic issues must be failures as mothers; and so we have the variously pathetic troupes of grotesquely neglected little Jellybys and "unnaturally constrained" young Pardiggles. Females, to Dickens, must be pretty and pleasant or they are not females, and every one of his books contains some expression of the compendium of his prejudices like this reflection upon the brother's widow in *Martin Chuzzlewit* (1844), who, "being almost supernaturally disagreeable, and having a dreary face, and a bony figure, and a masculine voice, was, in right of these qualities, what is commonly called a strong-minded woman" (Chapter IV).

Yet it is ironic to contemplate the vigour with which Dickens mocks the efforts of women who do conform to the contemporary social requirements. The daughters of the strong-minded woman affect the fashionable small waist, with the result, Dickens informs us mirthfully, that "sharp lacing was expressed in their very noses". And what are the odious Merry and Cherry,

118

daughters of Pecksniff in the same novel, but gross parodies of a type of female behaviour which Dickens elsewhere, without much shift of emphasis, invites us to admire? Perhaps the most interesting case here, though, is Esther Summerson. Her irritating oscillation between little girl and little old woman, indeed her entire existence in the diminutive which culminates in her being set up, without her knowledge or consent, in a miniature version of Bleak House at the end of the novel, has been much attacked by the critics; and today's reader will predictably recoil from her earnest morality, her coy ways, and her whole Girl Guide ethos. But does she deserve her creator's revenge, the blinding and disfigurement which are inflicted on her and only partially revoked, when her sight is restored almost in order that she may see and appreciate the blasting of her face?

Every literate person will recall other such examples from men's writing where prescriptive treatment alternates with punitive caricature; though not usually from such a distinguished pen as Dickens's. Female reaction to this has been predictable. Both as readers and as writers they have turned in large numbers to the consolations of romance, and have sought comfort and reassurance among the lower reaches of this ancient and venerable literary form. They have tended to abandon the larger issues, and have taken refuge in soothing dreams of happy marriage and life among the wealthy. Some women writers have tapped this vein of longing with beady-eyed calculation, and have grown rich on the profits—the Victorians and Edwardians seemed particularly ready to reward the purveyors of such stuff, as the careers of Marie Corelli, Ouida, and, later, Elinor Glyn will testify. But they also seem to have believed in what they were doing. Even the wonderful Mrs Amanda M'Kittrick Ros, the Queen of overblown romance writing and the female prose answer to the ineffable McGonagall, derived her potency, not to mention her receipts, from her ability to produce such passages as this without a glimmer of humour or self-consciousness. In this extract from her masterly *Irene Iddesleigh* (1897), p. 47, Sir John reproaches the divine Irene, who has, not to put too fine a point upon it, married him for his money:

I, you see, am tinged with slightly snowy tufts, the result of

119

a stifled sorrow and care concerning you alone; and on the memorable day of our alliance, as you are well aware, the black and glossy locks of glistening glory crowned my brow. There dwelt then, just six months this day, no trace of sorrow or smothered woe—no variety of colour where it is and shall be so long as I exist—no furrows of grief could then be traced upon my visage. But alas! now I feel so changed! And why?

Because I have dastardly and doggedly been made a tool of treason in the hands of the traitoress and unworthy! I was enticed to believe that an angel was always hovering around my footsteps, when moodily engaged in resolving to acquaint you of my great love, and undying desire to place you upon the highest pinnacle possible of praise and purity within my power to bestow!

I was led to believe that your unbounded joy and happiness were never at such a par as when sharing them with me. Was I falsely informed of your ways and worth? Was I duped to ascend the ladder of liberty, the hill of harmony, the tree of triumph, and the rock of regard, and when wildly manifesting my act of ascension, was I to be informed of treading still in the valley of defeat?

Am I, who for nearly forty years was idolised by a mother of untainted and great Christian bearing, to be treated now like a slave? Why and for what am I thus dealt with?

It is apparent that what we have here is not merely the preoccupation of an individual, but a flowering of a long-standing tradition based on a deep human need. The female character-type of romantic aspiration is classically rendered and shrewdly exposed by Hardy in his portrait of Eustacia in Chapter VII, Book I, of *The Return Of The Native* (1878). This young woman is developed entirely through her emotions and expressed, as it were, in a vacuum. She is never shown working, indeed she avoids anything remotely mundane in her determination to avoid compromising her self-image—a poignant cross-reference with the working girl Marty (an echo of the Biblical Martha?) in *The Woodlanders* (1887) is inevitable. Hardy does not spare the presentation of the other side of Eustacia's romantic nature, her shopgirl dreams of Paris, her idleness, her aspirations to be fashionable, all this the tawdry underslip to her superficial glamorous show. There is, too, a light but consistent ironising of her reliance upon paraphenalia, her telescope and her hourglass—she has a watch, but prefers the archaism, the evocation of a vanished but more gracious era (how readily the clichés come into play!).

But not only in character terms do we see the continuance of the tradition. The lure of romance is inherent in the novel form from the eighteenth century, and all too often in the twentieth what passes for serious fiction is in fact only a glorified and modishly revamped version of this staple. Partly this may be attributed to the continuing adherence to the older fictional modes, a consequence of the stress on the former styles of presenting external reality. Women writers as different as Pearl Buck and Olivia Manning carry on the tradition of books which provide a good solid read, constructed with a beginning, a middle, and an end, and offering some adventure, some love, and much reassurance. Even so recent a novel as Pamela Hansford Johnson's major opus, *The Survival Of The Fittest* (1968), is richly stuffed with instantly recognisable would-be romantic characters and scenes, within the framework as (so many times) before.

The story concerns a terrible writer of the Thirties literary crowd, a wild young boyo not even thinly disguised as Dylan Thomas. We are clearly intended to watch with love and sorrow his predictable career of self-destruction, as contrasted with that of his worthy but unsuccessful friend (this character must surely be one of those taken from stock which it is most difficult to bring off). To draw the civil leers to a close, it may be concluded that this type of fiction, which Pamela Hansford Johnson and her husband C. P. Snow are dedicated to preserving, has its place not only in the long history of English writing, but also in the hearts and minds of very many of the reading public. It is not, however, much, if anything, more than the extension of various historical precedents, and only a whisker divides it, at its worst from "romance" in the pejorative, the soothing and sentimental, sense of the term.

This is in fact for women writers the special danger, the particularised trap. Examples abound of the debasing of real issues to the "weak-sided" productions so blown up by Keats, even in the work of women writers whose reputations in their own day were not merely respectable but indeed towering. A classic case is that of Elizabeth Bowen, whose death in 1972 brought her fleetingly back into a limelight which she had not enjoyed for many years. Her gift lay in the evocation of the romance of class. In one of her main works, *The House in Paris* (1935), the parents of the heroine are described with approbation as "not only good to the poor, but kind to the common, tolerant of the intolerant". Theirs is a "world of grace and intelligence, in which the Boer War, the war, and other fatigues and disasters had been so many opportunities to behave well". This philosophy is also expressed in their attitude to their daughter's marriage, which is, naturally, synonymous with her entire destiny:

> Karen then saw that in [her mother's] view a woman's real life began only with marriage, that girlhood amounts to no more than a privileged looking on. Her own last four years showed up as rather aimless; it was true that her painting lately had been half-hearted; she seemed to have lost sight of her ambition. There is more art in simply living, Mrs Michaelis said. Karen was glad to fall back on her mother's view of things,
>
> (p. 60)

Inevitably Karen becomes involved with a man whom she has been brought up to regard as "a person who will not do". Max is French, Jewish, has "no family", and horror of horrors, *works* in a bank. Her mother greets the suggestion of their marrying with the opinion, "It would be horrible if it were a fact" (note the well-bred subjunctive). The author then outlines the way in which a subtle parent deals with a daughter in this situation:

> Not seeking husbands yet, they have no reason to love socially. This natural fleshly protest against good taste is broken down soon enough; their natural love of the cad is outwitted by their mothers. Vulgarity, inborn like original sin, unfolds with the woman's nature, unfolds ahead of it quickly and has a flamboyant flowering in the young girl. Wise mothers do not nip it immediately; that makes for trouble later; they watch it out.
>
> (p. 99)

This is very much the tone of the Thirties. A similar set of unexamined assumptions underlies the work of Rosamond Lehmann, though her subject-matter and technique are not otherwise comparable with those of Elizabeth Bowen. *The Weather In The Streets* (1936) seems to take Bowen's thesis a stage further when its heroine is actually shown as undertaking an affair with a "man who will not do". Rollo is disqualified not through any want of background, which is impeccable, as his name is chosen to indicate, but through the primary impediment of an existing marriage. The novel is divided into two sections of first-person narrative and two of third-person, and these movements are designed to coincide with and to convey the development of the love affair. We have first-person narrative when things are beginning and going well, while the retreat into third-person denotes the heroine's withdrawal, as the affair withers and shrinks, back into the emotional condition of listlessness and nervous inertia where we found her at the beginning. There is also use of a sort of stream-of-consciousness device. But strip the story of its fashionable fleshing down to the bare bones, and it is revealed as yet another saga of sensitive girl versus romantic irresistible sod, the game that was old when Byron played it. No matter how artfully done, it is still the same basic formula, the romance as before.

It is of course easy to mock and to "wrong the ancientry", and few productions of forty years ago will stand up against criticism informed by the massive socialisation of the common intelligence of the last decades. We are made uneasy, in our current obsession with the evil of assessment processes, by the novel of social prescription and indeed, social demarcation. Yet the romance novel does not need this sort of explanation or apology, for it heeds no check of changing literary directions and notices no rebuke from works of better standing. Such novels sail serenely in their thousands down the thirties and forties, yes; but there is no diminishing in their numbers along the years of the fifties, sixties, and even seventies.

It should be clear that we are not discussing commercial "romance" as written by (say) Denise Robbins and Barbara Cartland, but the work of women writers whose claim to be serious artists is not challenged and whose output will always command a decent measure of serious critical response. Enid Bagnold must be accounted a Grand Old Lady of English letters; yet her novel *The Loved And The Envied* (1951) shows how easily even an experienced and respected writer can succumb to the pull of romance writing. The heroine who is described by the title is beautiful, eternally youthful, quite irresistible, and happily surrounded by an assortment of other cliché characters—the silent but devoted lover, the hideous aunt who determines that her niece's beauty shall be her revenge on the world of men, the fortune-hunting gigolo in pursuit of the plain daughter, all these set against various arrogant aristocrats, faithful servants and wily peasants.

The assurance of the style in this novel is very marked. But it in no way distracts attention from the poverty of the material and its blatant appeal to the romance of class. Nearly all the characters are endowed with titles, land, money, social position, or at the least some cachet of talent or charm; and the significance of money in the novel's scale of values emerges from its importance in the conclusion, where the heroine, having worked through a husband and a daughter in the course of the novel, is left with a vast inheritance to renew her function and to take her into the happy-ever-after of the reader's envious fantasy. How totally such writing is based on the knowledge that those reading it will be infinitely poorer both than the characters in the novel, and than they themselves would like to be! (We cannot assume that real-life aristocrats would be flattered by reading the stuff, since their fictional counterparts are scarcely presented as literate, except in the matter of wills, deeds, and settlements.)

And so it goes on. One of the most successful of contemporary practitioners in this field is Elizabeth Jane Howard, who, despite her disparagement of "this childish equation of money with caste" in *The Sea Change* (1959), devotes most of her time in that novel to showing us precisely how and why it works. Her theme is not that money *is* caste, but that it will surely command the blessings and perquisites of caste, or where it cannot, it will operate very well in place of it. Her rich though humbly born playwright jets between London, New York, and a Greek holiday island; the lucky reader is treated to all the trappings of the romantic travelogue:

> We drive to Phaleron, past dusty squares where people drink orange soda under shrill strings of lights threaded through the tired trees: down one long narrow street which had at its end and above us the Acropolis, radiant in the full dress of flood-lighting—out on to a wide highway where one notices chiefly the evening sky with land dark below it pollinated with lights. We turn on to a road which has the harbour on our left—the waters

have still a dull sheen on them from the sun—like golden oil. There are a few boats anchored and an air of gentle desertion, but to our right, cafés, booths, restaurants are strung out with irregular bursts of cheap savage light and violent music. As we climb, the curve of Phaleron is below us to our left; pretty, laid out with beady lights like a doll's bay which blots out as we plunge into the quiet town above it.

(p. 231)

Meanwhile two women, one old and sensitive, one young and fresh, circulate around the sixty-year-old writer. His wife is shown as loving her husband and dead child too much, and suffers from heart trouble(note the cunning metaphor here)—her role is defined as "not doing anything particular, but just being someone". Being it elegantly and graciously, of course—*Aida* on the radiogram, drinks at the ready, and always, always, the faultless sartorial effect: "She was wearing a long dress of some finely pleated material—a very dark blue—bare on one shoulder and caught on the other by a swag of wonderful pearls . . . her face and all her skin had the most astonishing radiance, and her hair looked as though there was moonlight on it". The echo of Fitzgerald's immortal *The Great Gatsby* (1925) only heightens the unfortunate discrepancy between this and genuinely fine romance writing.

It is interesting to observe that among the effects sought by this type of writing is the stimulation of nostalgia, the wistful feeling that they don't write about women like that any more, when in fact they do. Of course they do; the genre is indestructible. One final example of the current model, updated in certain details but unchanged as to the reliable central formula, is Elizabeth Jenkins' *Honey* (1968). This is yet another story of a breathlessly beautiful, quite irresistible, totally uninteresting female character, so much so that the reader will frequently suspect that it must be a satire until conclusively denied that possibility. The novel offers itself, indeed, as a piece of realistic writing, down to the "trendy documentary" style of observation, of clothes, houses, and domestic details that we have become used to; yet at the core of this "realism" moves our old friend, La Belle Dame Sans Merci, the fantasy figure of the beautiful woman who simply cannot fail, but cannot love: "Wherever she was, some man was at

125

hand, begging to be allowed to spend his money on her"—"Every man who saw Honey was strongly attracted by her". Sadly, this could have been a better novel, had its centre been shifted from the meaningless Honey to the other family which it deals with, the Cresswells. This family too is rendered cloying by having in its midst as wife and mother another super-female in a different way, the "superb cook" stereotype. But theirs is at least a convincing story of normal family interaction, unlike the stale dream which is Honey. Too many writers of this type seem to think of their readers in terms of the "damp souls" which T. S. Eliot remarked so condescendingly in housemaids, with predictable results.

When so much of the creative energy of women writers is devoted to the romanticisation of class, or its equivalent, money, it follows that there will inevitably be a derogation of those less well endowed in social and financial matters. Up to a point most writers cannot avoid being the educated observer by virtue of their upbringing and circumstances. But it is how and what is observed and recorded that we react to. Doris Lessing's treatment of working people in *The Golden Notebook* makes this point. With all its vital virtues this much-acclaimed novel is in many ways an enchanted circle book. Molly, one of the main characters, speaks "half a dozen languages well", and has more than her share of other talents, "painting and dancing and acting and scribbling". Anna, her friend and the novel's central character, has written an important first novel on the topical subject of South Africa (as Doris Lessing herself did). Her lovers are a doctor and a writer, and she mixes in "artistic circles". Molly's ex-husband Richard is a big tycoon; the nearest character to the ordinary is Richard's untalented current wife Marion, who is "treated like a house-wife or hostess, but never as a human being".

For all their socialism, Molly and Anna are rooted in the old forms. Their children both go away to school, and Richard, though despised as a "jumped-up grocer" is yet admiringly categorised as "one of the financial powers of the country", "a big shot". He not only pays the school fees of a son he rarely sees and cannot get on with, but is also expected by the women to find the boy a place in one of his business concerns, something that "isn't just share-pushing or promoting or money-making"—something, that is, not too nakedly commercial, to spare the Communist Party souls of Molly and her son. Elsewhere, abortive encounters with the milkman and a barrowboy emphasise Molly's inability to live her socialism, despite her scorn of "working-class Tories".

Yet for all this, Doris Lessing's treatment of these working men is strongly contrasted with the traditional treatment of the lower orders in British fiction of this century. They are usually used as walking exempla of the coarse-grained, brought on to highlight the emotional and even physical delicacy of the principal characters, or else to illustrate with the solecisms of the half-educated the understated elegance and rightness of the characters' or author's style. Elizabeth Bowen's Karen expresses it with brutal directness: "Servants are terrible: why should they share one's house?" Such a violent aversion to social inferiors is not common in twentieth-century fiction. Nevertheless, it is extremely rare that the novelist of either sex truly feels in and with a lower-class man or woman. The most typical way of dealing with such characters is via the nineteenth-century mode of external observation and recording. This is exemplified in Ivy Compton-Burnett's memories of her girlhood:

> I remember a thing happening that couldn't possibly happen now. The manservant used to roar out the hymns in a very loud voice, and the cook—that particular cook we had then was a woman my mother was afraid of, my mother was a woman who feared neither God nor man, but she did fear that cook—and that cook liked singing. She was a Plymouth brother, and she was always singing hymns, and one of her temperance hymns was "I'll drink his water bright". Well, she used to like these weekly prayers, you see, and she used to love singing, but the manservant drowned her voice and my mother said, "Harvey, try to keep your voice back a little, you drown the women's voices." "Very good 'um", he said. And my mother said, "Harvey, don't say very good 'um. I'm always telling you to say, 'Yes, very good 'um'." I always remember that scene.
>
> (*Ivy and Stevie*, pp. 4–5)

This tone, of pleased amusement at the antics of the human zoo, tends to remain in force today. The so-called "working-class novels" of the later nineteen-fifties and early sixties—*Satur-*

day Night and Sunday Morning, A Kind Of Loving, The Loneliness of the Long-Distance Runner—may have gone some way towards restoring to working people that dignity and significance which they have often been denied, in literature as in life.[1] But such people still tend to receive full-length presentation only when shown in action upon their own ground. Seen in terms of working for someone else, or outside the domestic relationship, they frequently remain comic and semi-developed, where they exist at all. They are not common characters.

Margaret Forster's heroine, in *The Travels of Maudie Tipstaff* (1967), is one of the rare working-class characters studied in depth by modern women writers. Yet this when analysed is not the portrait that we might expect. The character is very much drawn from outside, and all the working-class stereotypes are mustered up in the characterisation; she is old, but not giving in yet, careful with money to the point of miserliness, proud, rigid, disgusted by sex and sloppiness, emotionally and linguistically impoverished to the point of caricature. The final effect, though surely not intended, is one of condescension. The situations seem too patently contrived to display this or that feature.

The same is true of the travels around which the novel is constructed. Maudie progresses from one of her children to another in a calculated and barely credible series of contrasts and appositions. Jean, her eldest, is respectably married to a dentist, and living in suburban comfort in Golders Green. Jean has one child, a well-bred fifteen-year-old at boarding school, produced with an effort which has deterred the couple from further attempts. They holiday in Greece, and think nothing of spending hundreds of pounds on an attic conversion so that Maudie can have her own self-contained flat. Jean is at odds with her husband, who is mildly unfaithful in the suburban style; she is unsatisfied with the golf club, coffee-morning level of her existence; and she fears her mother.

Sally, in diagrammatic contrast, is loosely married to a farm labourer and lives in a tiny agricultural worker's cottage in the heart of the Northern Dales. She has six children and becomes

[1] See Nigel Gray's *The Silent Majority: A Study of the Working Class in Post-war British Fiction* (1973).

pregnant with another during Maudie's stay; she teems readily and unfussily, like an animal. Her husband is poorly paid, and Sally is a shiftless, thriftless manager. She loves her husband and all the world, doubling as the local harlot in her spare time; she smokes, slops around, and never scrubs her floors. She even forgets to baste the meat so that it dries out (a perfect example, this, of the author's method, expecting the reader to identify with Maudie on issues so patently silly). Sally is warm where Jean is cold; lickerish where Jean is frustrated and inadequate; careless against Jean's fastidiousness; poor against Jean's comfortable circumstances. The novel reads as if the two girls were constructed from lists of opposites, and tailored to clash with Maudie's character on all points.

And clash they do. At the end of the story, Maudie has learned as her lesson the thumping cliché that "everyone is on their own". Yet in the novel's epilogue we leave her preparing to embark on her travels again, on the grounds that however unpleasant it all was, travelling is "better than staying here". This seems to be an unpenetrating and unsatisfactory conclusion. But in fairness, some at least of the difficulty must be located in the source material from which Margaret Forster is working. There are a whole series of technical problems for the educated writer today in the satis-factory presentation of these characters, and it is admittedly ex-tremely hard to avoid the reduction of them to a comic or elegiac tribe of extras such as we turn to Hardy to enjoy.

Even Iris Murdoch, whose stress on the uniqueness of every individual forms the philosophic basis of all her work, is not exempt from the fairly general failure to resolve this dilemma. She has recorded her respect for Shakespeare's enormously varied yet faithful and considerate character-drawing. This is a harsh self-comparison, which no writer could withstand, yet even on a lower level it is hard to feel anything but embarrassed by the portrait of Mrs Carberry, the daily woman in *An Accidental Man* (1971), additionally handicapped as she is by the possession of a retarded son. This gruesome twosome recalls Oscar Wilde's re-mark about the death of Little Nell, that one would have to have a heart of stone, to read it without laughing. The comicality here, though, is surely to be seen as a failure of tone or technique rather than in any way as a conscious belittlement or deliberate expression of élitist values. The refutation of any such charge lies in an earlier study, that of Pattie in *The Time Of The Angels* (1966). This woman—servant, housekeeper, lover, black Madonna to the mad and terrible Carel in the deserted Rectory—is a superb study of the psychology of service, the emotional mechanism which ensures that the coals will still be brought in even though the house is (literally) about to come down. The warmth and immediacy with which Pattie is brought before us, the compassionate but complete demonstration of her inadequacy, her devotion, and her misery, make this an entirely vivid and convincing character-study; and at the same time, they lift it to something more, so that Pattie, in all her rarity, stands for all those who have known what it is to perform hard and humiliating work without anything like sufficient spiritual or financial recompense.

We have seen that the central problem for the novel in the twentieth century has been the relation between what separated out as "individual" or "psychological" fiction on the one hand, and "social" or "general" on the other. There has occurred a division of matter and method in the novel between the individual and the society, the public and the private, the social and the literary. The choice between these alternatives has joined, and I would think influenced to a degree, all the other choices which are involved in the act of creation. Stress on certain subjects automatically rules out consideration of others; trouble with the servants pales in conjunction with war, poverty, revolution, bloodshed; will not in fact inhabit the same fictional sector except as a nuisance or an irrelevance, unless the writer is Tolstoy. The concentration by many women writers upon the domestic front has meant that they have not frequently, or very notably, got to grips with what are generally regarded as the "big" issues— war, politics, madness, crime. It is interesting to ask why these themes seem so much more important than more homely fictional topics. The ultra-feminist would say that it is because they have, excluding madness, been for many centuries masculine provinces, and accordingly take on superior status from this association. More plausibly we might suggest that it is because they form the staple of, and probably receive their definitive treatment in, the

Russian novel of the nineteenth century, from whose intimidating aspect Western cultural intelligence is even yet recovering.

Whatever the explanation, it is true that women writers have tended to shy away from much effort to represent war. The apparently obvious exception to this statement, Margaret Mitchell's *Gone With The Wind* (1936), reveals itself on inspection to be a romance with a backdrop of hostilities, a story in which the fighting is used to add tension and interest to the actions of the principals. The same is true of Iris Murdoch's account of the Irish troubles, *The Red And The Green* (1965). It is significant in this discussion that the war novel of Elizabeth Bowen which was most highly praised when it appeared, and which some critics regard as her masterpiece, *The Heat Of The Day* (1949), deals in fact with the lives and actions of a group of people who did not go to the war, but stayed at home. Among more recent novels on this front, Susan Hill's *Strange Meeting* (1971) reads like an example of that worthy and familiar form so long ago claimed by women writers and declared to be female territory, the historical novel. The allusion in the title to Wilfred Owen's magnificent First World War poem is unfortunate as it draws attention to the distance between a genuine, brilliant, and moving production of that terrible time, and a return to it which is essentially and apparently a modern artefact. Susan Hill goes to unnecessary pains to avoid any homosexual or even emotional colouring in her handling of the developing love between two young officers at the front. This, taken with the fact that the hero is a classic of the type that E. M. Forster made his own, the unawakened heart, makes for a certain coldness, a lack of engagement about the whole thing, despite some would-be vigorous trench details, of smells, and wounds, and rats.

The convulsions of society in one of its periodic outbursts of uncontrolled violence may require all the skills of a Tolstoy to render it acceptably; and lesser writers of either sex may understandably quail before the task. But it is remarkable that so little interest, relatively speaking, has been shown in the operations of society in that state of controlled violence which we call peacetime. Many readers would agree with Stendhal (*The Charterhouse of Parma*, 1839, Chapter XXIII), that "politics in a work of literature are like a pistol shot in the middle of a concert, something loud and vulgar and yet a thing to which it is not possible to refuse one's attention". This may link with many "lady novelists' " fear of vulgarity and concentration upon the safe and soothing to explain the absence of comment upon anything that might remotely be described as political in novels written by women.

In view of this *lacuna*, Winifred Holtby's *South Riding* (1936) deserves an honourable mention in respect of its aims, if not its achievements. It is one of the few works of fiction which deal at length with the machinery of local government, without attempting to make humorous capital out of its shortcomings. We are shown the councillors in session, and in private life; the writer, whose material was drawn from the experiences of her own mother as an alderman and mayor, tries fairly to give some sense of the inter-party tensions and parochial bickering that we expect of local government, and yet to convey the fact that a decision confronting such people may not be any the less difficult or important because it concerns a local matter.

Nor is this the limit of Winifred Holtby's interest in politics. Surprisingly, in view of the fact that it is an intensely conventional work, there is an insistent feminist note sounded throughout, mainly through the character of the emancipated young headmistress, Miss Burton, many of whose arguments remain depressingly relevant today. We have, too, an early association of the cause of women with that of other oppressed groups, principally the negroes (this again is reminiscent of the origins of the modern women's liberation movement in America). Here is Sarah Burton defending her point of view against a traditionally-minded male:

> You know the story of the difference between the North and South Americans and their attitude towards the negroes? The Southerner says: "You're a slave, God bless you"; the Northerner: "You're a free man, damn you!" I remember how a man I used to know in South Africa said he loved the natives. He was an Afrikaans farmer who believed in flogging blacks for breaches of the Masters and Servants Act . . . I hate this feudal love in which there's no give and take. "I love the ladies." "I love my labourers." Love needs the stiffening of respect, the give and take of equality.
>
> (Book Two, Chapter Four)

Apart from this, the reader whose tastes lie that way has very much to peck about to find any grains of political matter in the mass of fiction turned out every year. Most women, it seems, would rather write *Grand Hotel, The Daughter Of Time*, or *The Murder of Roger Ackroyd*, or even nothing, than write anything which may bear comparison with some of the political novels for which America or Germany is famous. The theme is present, as is so much else, in Carson McCullers's *The Heart Is A Lonely Hunter* (1943), and handled with characteristic use of resonant allusion and luminous detail. In the McCullers universe, politics provide yet another arena in which human ideals and aspirations are pitifully measured against human weakness and wickedness. The black doctor, Copeland, one of the main characters, embodies a series of paradoxes—he is a healer, yet dying of tuberculosis; he is intensly proud yet forced to endure the routine contempt of every white man; he is a committed father, yet estranged from his children. His politics naturally fit in with this pattern of longing and disappointment. His passionate vision of socialism yet denies the true (and the social) nature of his own race; his christening his son Karl Marx signifies his ideal, but shows too how he unknowingly undermines it by his determination to Westernise his people at all costs, even at the price of their ethnic identity. The foundering of his hopes is indicated, with poetic economy and poignance of effect, by the fact that his son is never called anything but "Buddy", itself an ironic comment upon the inability of human beings to entertain anything but the false outward show, the nomenclature, of friendship and brotherhood.

Parallel with Copeland stands the itinerant labourer, Jake. He has no history, and is "one of the people" in the basic sense that he simply emerges from the slow swell of humanity into the foreground of the narrative with all his ordinariness and all his singularity on his back. He has no cash, no capital, no house, no land; he works for his livelihood, and believes in his work and his fellow-workers; but the failure of *his* brand of socialism is revealed through his failure to mobilise, or even to get on with, his fellows. Finally, just before Jake disappears from the story, hitting the road out of town like so many characters in American fiction, he is repeatedly brought into contact with a mad evangelist, a ludicrous and unregarded prophet of primitive

133

Christianity. In this crushing association we are given a glimpse by the author of how Jake appears to the millions who have no time or use for his "message".

The final effect of the novel is not so melancholy as this summary might suggest. Copeland, Jake, and the other characters all revolve around one man, Singer. Singer, who is gifted with great grace, sweetness, and fidelity, and handicapped by being congenitally mute, stands for the richness of human love, and also the mystery of limitation and incomprehension which lies at its heart. He loves and is loved, as do the other characters in their own ways. But none understands him, nor he them, nor do these varied impulses of love manage to coincide or even coexist. The habit of the imperfect lover to adopt only those aspects of the beloved with which he can identify is expressed in the simple point that Copeland believes Singer to be Jewish and hence a member, like him, of an ancient and abused race, while Jake, who is constantly linked with the Irish, claims Singer as Irish too. In this way Singer offers, however unconsciously, to each what he can take, and after his death his legacy is one of goodness. As his love for his friend Antanopoulos began the novel, so Carson McCullers draws to a close by showing how the thoughts of another character, at Singer's funeral, bring him to a vision of love between individual people set against "the endless fluid passage of humanity through endless time". So we must walk, is the conclusion, somewhere "between irony and faith", with no reliance upon political theories or structures but guided by the dictates of what she elsewhere called "the mortgaged heart".

In any consideration of the importance of politics in the work of women writers, the name of Ivy Compton-Burnett irresistibly suggests itself. This ostensibly ultraconventional writer, who observes so scrupulously most of the country-house traditions of English fiction, is arguably the most political of writers on the twentieth-century scene. Her radicalism is expressed through a series of attacks upon figures of authority and accepted social structures. Her rejection of the sanctity of conventional sexual roles has already been discussed; I would like to link it up at this point with her general feeling that no person or institution can stand up to scrutiny. Mary McCarthy has drawn attention to the centrality of the themes of nature and equality in her work, and to her ever-present sense of the lives of the underprivileged which is implied in her pitiless censure of the egotistical self-absorption of the well-off.

It would be a false sentimentalisation to pretend that Ivy ever really understood or cared warmly for the servants in her fiction. But in so far as she is inclined to make allowances for anyone, she does tend to suggest that where those who have had every advantage of wealth and position cannot conduct themselves in a civilised way, how much less should we expect of one who has had little, and lives in daily contact with those who have had much. Her servants have this further importance, too, that so far from being archaic survivors from a forgotten world, they are in fact metaphors of an enduring human situation. We are all, by the nature of society itself, imprisoned in a hierarchical structure; we are all, willy-nilly, superior to some and inferior to others. It is how we define "superior" and "inferior" which defines us.

She illustrates this point through her presentation of various social groups which usually command some respect. Foremost among those to feel the lash are the purveyors of Christianity. Many critics have remarked on the incidence of creepy clergymen in her work. Notice the malicious suggestiveness of the naming of Oscar Jekyll, the vicar without faith in *A House And Its Head* (1935). The pompous and untrustworthy Edward in *Brothers and Sisters* (1950) is another apparent indication of her belief that those whom the faithful look to for guidance are themselves stumbling in the dark; not only this, they are inevitably hypocrites, because, in the nature of their work, they are pretending to know the way. Ivy spares neither the deceiver nor the deceived. In yet another of those surprising but very real flashes of affinity with Mary McCarthy, she seems to believe, in McCarthy's phrase, that "religion is for peasants", and that anyone above peasant who engages themselves with it is conniving at the administering of a great communal placebo; or worse, serving themselves in the fiction of serving God. Such a one is the spurious, sickly-sweet Beatrice Fellows, also in *A House And Its Head*, who makes a life's work out of going round her "fellows" with her "simple little messages of Christianity", whether people want them or not.

135

This disregard of the true need of those around in favour of a scheme of belief preferred by the giver, links the clergy with another prominent social group in the Compton-Burnett universe, as the title of her 1925 novel indicates: *Pastors and Masters*. The teachers in this novel are assessed in terms of the two wings of their profession; they are seen as creators, "Poets", in the Greek sense of the word, and hence are compared with writers; they are also considered as spiritual mentors, and, in this role, they are compared with vicars (there are two writers and two vicars in the novel). The central character, mockingly called Herrick after the playful Cavalier poet, is both a writer, and, as the owner of the school, a teacher too; he insists on reading the Lesson every morning in assembly, to abrogate to himself a religious and pastoral function. His claims in all these departments are however shown to be hollow, and he is involved in the ultimate intellectual hypocrisy when he attempts to plagiarise another man's work.

Hollowness is in fact the general failing of these educators. All the other characters in the novel who are likewise engaged in the care of the young are shown to be shoddy fakes, imposing upon the ignorant credulity of the inexperienced or undiscerning. Here Ivy Compton-Burnett demonstrates the meanness, intellectual poverty, and reflex sarcasm of the inadequate teacher:

> Well, this is a nice thing! A nice thing this schoolmastering! Up at seven and in a room with a black fire. . . . I should have thought it might have occurred to one out of forty boys to poke it. . . ."
>
> (p. 7)

Another dreadful example is presented in the person of Richard Bumpus, an Oxford Fellow, and another plagiarist (dare we suspect Ivy of indecent punning intent in the naming of this homosexual?). Finally it is worth observing that none of Ivy Compton-Burnett's teachers has more than an imperfect or half-realised relationship with any one of either sex; teachers are, she suggests, incomplete human beings.

But school, as one of her characters reflects in *The Mighty And Their Fall*, "cannot have the fine edge of family life". It is in and through the family that Ivy Compton-Burnett sees the

136

socialisation of the individual being accomplished, at whatever private cost. This writer's habit of invariably setting her stories around a family or two is potentially rather misleading, and today's critics usually begin by observing how traditional this is in the English novel in such a way as to suggest that her subject-matter is correspondingly remote. But is it so archaic that she places her characters in this milieu? Many social conventions have been relaxed only to give way to others which are differently but no less rigid. We are all fated to inhabit some social structure; we are all born into, and usually live and die in, families; and the modern family has lost none of its primitive power to damage and to deform.

Ivy herself always asserted that what she called "the important things" do not change, that human nature does not change. Social and personal forces act upon us now as they did in the "1885" which is her perennial timescape. She felt too that her work had the permanent relevance of any achieved work of art. She told Kay Dick in conversation, "I haven't written any rubbish", and further claimed herself to be "quite perfect morally". As this suggests, she saw her work as both relevant and important, and herself as concerned with the most serious aspects of human life. In her often-quoted remark, "people have a way of not coming out well in a temptation. They generally behave quite as ill as they can." Set this against her dogmatic belief that "you must recognise certain moral laws. Otherwise you couldn't have any human life, any literature or anything." These statements, couched in the characteristically sparse Compton-Burnett vocabulary, terse as they are, fully indicate the range and scope of her vision of life.

This sense of the profounder issues of contemporary society is one that Ivy Compton-Burnett has shared with several other important women writers of the twentieth century. While it is true that women on the whole tend to avoid the "big" themes of war, madness, crime, they do not as a result give us nothing more exciting than a literary tea party. Perhaps in continuation of their role of the "angel at the hearth" and guardian of spiritual well-being, women writers have always concerned themselves strongly with moral themes. They have constantly sought in their fiction a definition of the means by which human beings may live properly together. This concern has not always been expressed in family and parochial terms. Doris Lessing, in her first novel, *The Grass Is Singing* (1950), confronts a problem which has increased in magnitude during the decades following the book's publication, that of race. She tells the story of Mary, an undiscerning and limited woman married to a poor white South African farmer; given the weak foundation of the relationship between them, and the tensions produced by the difficulties of working the farm, the tragic conclusion is inevitable. They have married on the strength of unreal and delusive visions of each other; both are ordinary mortals, as their names, Mary and Dick, signify, yet each sees and expects an illusory glamour in the other. Through Mary, Doris Lessing attacks the burden that is placed upon women by the social expectation that they must marry, or be accounted failures. Mary's weaknesses are fully detailed, but she is also presented as a victim of her culture and society: "All women become conscious, sooner or later, of that impalpable, but steel-strong pressure to get married." Mary marries to fulfil a social obligation, not as an overwhelming desire to spend the rest of her life with Dick.

This novel is not only Mary's story. Its unsung hero is "the native", brought into prominence first through Mary's inability to deal with those whose situation is, ironically, in some ways analogous with hers. This affinity is partly suggested through the language difficulty—Mary's reluctance to learn "kitchen kaffir" in order to be able to speak with the natives symbolises her awkwardness of communication with all people, and her inability to make the effort to meet them in conversation. Partly, too, her relations with the natives are warped, from the start, by her regarding them with the distorting perspective of the white view, here sardonically outlined by Lessing (pp. 92–3):

> Whenever two or three farmers are gathered together, it is decreed that they should discuss nothing but the shortcomings and deficiencies of their natives. They talk about the labourers with a persistent irritation sounding in their voices: individual natives they might like, but as a genus, they loathe them. They loathe them to the point of neurosis. They never cease complaining about their unhappy lot, having to deal with natives who are so exasperatingly

indifferent to the welfare of the white man, working only to please themselves. They had no idea of the dignity of labour, no idea of improving themselves by hard work.

Mary feels herself to be cheated and downtrodden by this life. But when, through her husband's illness, she takes over the running of the farm and the management of the natives, she discovers within herself the attitudes of the oppressor in the heart of the oppressed. She lashes a native across the face with a *sjambok*, a climactic moment which is rendered with an almost disgusting vividness: "A thick weal pushed up along the dark skin of the cheek as she looked, and from it a drop of bright blood gathered and trickled down and off his chin, and splashed to his chest." This infliction of the wound establishes an unbreakable bond between them—she always recognises this native by his scar, in defiance of the natural law which dictates that one black looks like another to a white woman. This man, symbolically named Moses, assumes greater and greater importance in Mary's life. As she goes mad and "rotten", her mental horizon narrows until all her being is concentrated upon this one native, who comes to be both her life and death to her.

Like all ambitious first works, *The Grass Is Singing* is not without its stereotyped moments, even in those areas where it passes over relatively untrodden ground, the life and behaviour of "the native", for instance. Moses is "a great hulk of a man", possessed of "some dark attraction". Mary feels "helplessly in his power", and he asserts a sub-Lawrentian authority over her. He develops an "easy, confident, bullying insolence", and she is subdued by his "conscious power", "the superior sexual potency of the native". Doris Lessing presents him increasingly through his physical presence, and he impinges on Mary's weakening mind more and more as a force than as a person. She moves him in and out of the action, rarely allowing him to say anything, wisely, perhaps, when one of his few permitted conversational sallies is, "Did Jesus think it right that people should kill each other?" Eventually, however, Moses is successfully brought through not as a human individual but as part of the nightmare in which Mary is swallowed up.

Something similar is achieved through the use of the desert in this novel. Initially it is a real, physical landscape, on and in which

Mary has to live. But subtly and gradually, as her hopes fail like a doomed springtime crop, the desert becomes a symbolic landscape as well, its aridity internalised, its vast wastes an external reproach commensurate with her own inner devastation. This fearful symbol never ceased to haunt Doris Lessing's imagination, even years after leaving her native South Africa for the cold and damp of London. The breakdown of Anna, heroine of *The Golden Notebook*, is shot through with this image; her fantasy of personal and literary sterility finds its worst and most crippling expression in her dreams of the desert, parched and cracked. The desert in the South African stories also exerts its power over those who live on it, even those who think to master it by growing rich from it. Much of her early work is concerned with attacking the dryness of the Colony way of life, with its petty pretensions, its restrictions, and its overheated response to the pervasive irrational dread of "the kaffir".

Despite its sometimes plodding realism, the doggedly accurate re-creation of the very grain of life in the bush, Doris Lessing's African fiction attains at its best an impressive respect and fidelity towards the natives that it deals with. Doris Lessing is, however, writing of the as yet comparatively undeveloped black of the South African bush and farm, and her focus is specifically on his relationship with his white "bosses". She rarely gives us black characters on their own, quite away from whites, and as a result we see little of the negroes' characteristic racial culturation. Her black man is perpetually a "kaffir", presented as he exists to white South African eyes, an inferior version of humanity because first moulded, and then judged and rejected, by an alien and hostile white culture. A different method is to be observed in Carson McCullers's treatment of the black inhabitants of southern America. It has frequently been noted that the negroes in Carson McCullers's fiction are deeply integrated into her view of life. Indeed, she is unique in her ability to show negro characters as they are to and with each other, and not only in their relations with whites, however sympathetically that may be done. McCullers never underrated the special quality of being black in the South; she renders it in its own authentic speech in such a way as to capture the blackness, but not *only* the blackness, of the southern American negro life. It is significant to recall here that Mc-

Cullers ascribes Dr Copeland's failure to his refusal to recognise his race's peculiar cultural needs; and she never stresses the special negro qualities at the expense of their right to a share in the characteristic business of being human.

The business of being human means, for Carson McCullers, an inescapable involvement with the rhythms of love and death, shown constantly in alteration and alternation, sometimes each expressed as either. It is this ability to represent archetypal human passions in their continuous everyday motion which gives Carson McCullers's work its mythic power. In the life of the negro the flux and reflux of emotion and event is given an added urgency by the uncertainty of their jobs, their houses, their security in short. None knows where or when the blow will fall. Carson McCullers patterns out her stark view of their prospects in the very structure of her novels, which usually contain a series of escalating disasters for the black characters, or, at the very best, no improvement in prospects, however vital or sanguine each individual may be.

A brief look at one example will illustrate this. Who could forget the wonderful Berenice in *The Member Of The Wedding* (1947), seen first in her pride with her oddly assorted male companions "T.T.", and her "lavender coloured" foster-brother Honey? Yet within a few weeks her small and undemanding life is dissolved by the imprisonment of Honey, the agonising death of her six-year-old charge, John Henry, and the removal of the white family she works for to a new home where she will not be wanted. The sole course of action open to her is marriage to T.T., who although "a proper man" and well-off, lacks the one quality that Berenice looks for in a man—"He don't make me shiver none". This unforgettable family, like that in *The Heart Is A Lonely Hunter*, is drawn with such profundity, grace, and strength, as ultimately to offer a world in itself. The work of Carson McCullers constantly suggests this hypothesis, that it is in the negro life and culture that what Henry James called the missing dimension of American society and fiction is to be found, the deepening of the perspective which he felt that English life derived from its inheritance of aristocracy, clergy, and so on.

It is to some extent a falsification to attempt to isolate any one feature in the work of so varied and strange a writer as McCullers;

141

but among the springs of her sensibility that never fail, prominent is her feeling for any undefended and half-articulate creature making its erratic and slippery way through life. As is to be expected hers are among the most successful efforts in contemporary fiction to represent the experiences and emotional development of childhood. She knows what most of us have suppressed, that a child's growth does not occur in a steady progression, but in wild and usually painful spurts, where the child's previous formula of life, or satisfaction with his achievements, is abruptly broken, and a bewildering new idea of reality replaces the previous and itself imperfectly assimilated version.

Frankie's story, in *The Member Of The Wedding*, is that of any young being. Indeed, its breadth of understanding is such that we should not even restrict it by categorising it as a portrait of a young female. Notice how wryly Carson McCullers catches in Frankie the close correspondence of comedy and pathos in the behaviour of the human young. Frankie is tormented with a fear of smelling which causes her to advertise her personal daintiness to all the world—" 'Boy!' she said. 'I bet I use more perfume than anybody in this town.' " Her other fears, of exclusion from the select gang of older ones, of growing too tall, of sexual experience, of being "found out" by the police, of her own aimlessness, are ruefully recognisable as the commonplace tortures of adolescence, but given here with a total freshness and precision, and carrying an unassailable conviction. It seems to me that Carson McCullers is so successful with this child because she does not see her as a child. Her primary theme, and one which she pursues quite consistently throughout her work, is the still sad music of humanity in all its variations, and the loneliness that that entails. Her aim here is to give us the development of a consciousness, not a snapshot of a little child. But it is also her strength that the more she concentrates upon the individual, the parochial even, the more we find her novels opening up as fables and assuming the status of timeless, placeless narratives located only somewhere in the eternal swell of human experience.

Of all contemporary women novelists, though, the writer who is most whole-heartedly concerned with moral themes is Iris Murdoch. As her nonfictional philosophical writings make clear, she is interested to assert and to explicate "the sovereignty of good", in the title phrase of her essay on the subject. She is aware that it is hardly a fashionable preoccupation; as she drily observes, "It is significant that the idea of goodness and of virtue has been largely superseded in Western moral philosophy by the idea of rightness, supported perhaps by some conception of sincerity". She is not seeking simply to reverse this trend by a plain statement of her beliefs and an attack upon those who do not conform to them as "trimmers, time-servers, toadies, compromisers, comfort-lovers, any of the varieties of coward", in Mary McCarthy's style (*Observer Review*, 19 December 1971). Her method, and the magnitude of her task, is nearer to that reflected upon by Dostoevsky in his preliminary comments upon *The Idiot* (1886):

> The idea of the novel is my old favourite idea, but so difficult that I for long did not dare to attempt it; and if I have attempted it now it is certainly because I found myself in a desperate situation. The principal conception of the novel is to depict the positively good man. There is nothing in the world more difficult, particularly nowadays. Of all writers (not merely our own, but European writers too), those who have attempted to depict the positively good have always missed the mark. For it is an infinite task. The good is an ideal, and both our ideal and that of civilised Europe is still far from having been worked out. In the whole world there is only one positively good man, Christ. . . . Of the good types in Christian literature, the most perfect is Don Quixote. But he is good only because at the same time he is ridiculous. The Pickwick of Dickens (an infinitely weaker conception than Don Quixote, but still immense) is also ridiculous and succeeds in virtue of this. A feeling of compassion is produced for the much ridiculed good man who does not know his own worth, and thus perhaps sympathy is evoked in the reader. This rousing of compassion is the secret of humour.
>
> (E. H. Carr, *Dostoevsky 1821–1881*, 1931; 1962 edition, pp. 159–60)

If Dostoevsky's theory, that compassion and humour are near kin, provides any bearing upon Iris Murdoch's work, then it is one that is sorely needed. It is characteristic of this writer that her methods and materials are so diverse as to dazzle and befuddle her readers. First, there is her interest in a variety of forms;

her critics have remarked a tendency to parody the romantic, the Gothic, or whatever, but it seems more likely that she is simply intending to exercise her considerable skill in the use and management of certain classic fictional genres. Consider *The Nice And The Good* (1968), which begins with a shot in Whitehall and an uncharacteristic rustle in the corridors of power. Any fan of the detective novel will feel at home with sequences like these:

> He moved round the desk on the side away from Radeechy's face and leaning over the chair saw a round hole in the back of the head, a little to the right of the slight depression at the base of the skull. The hole was quite large, a dark orifice with blackened edges. A little blood, not much, had run down inside the collar.

> (pp. 8–9)

Similarly readers of *The Unicorn* (1969) will not query Hannah's refusal or inability to leave the remote dwelling where she is some kind of prisoner, to put it no higher; it is a convention of Gothic fiction that the princess is and must be in the tower, and she is not usually asked whether she wants to be there or not.

Another diverting and distracting feature of this writer is her rich allusiveness, which springs from her inexhaustible interest in word and symbol. The basis of communication may be language but everyone means and understands differently from everyone else, sometimes to such an extent that a communication failure will involve the reduction of personality in the people concerned. Thus David Levkin, the Russian Jew who cannot even get his name pronounced properly in England, expresses his feelings: "Nothing means anything to me outside Russia. Your language is dry, dry in my mouth. Here I am a non-man" (*The Italian Girl*, 1964, p. 189). It is perhaps in this light that we should interpret what have been regarded as artistic defects, the occasional lapses into what A. S. Byatt calls her "sloppy style", her woman's novel style. When she makes a character cry out such reverberant lines as "Coward and fool! . . . You have made your own future!" (*The Sandcastle*, 1957, p. 312), we are surely not to suppose that Iris Murdoch is unaware of the tone here. More probably, she is seeking to convey a common human weakness, the tendency to try to elevate life's little moments into full melodrama by resort to Rattiganesque attitudinising phraseology. Language, which should further communication, commonly retards it by providing us with a vehicle which we use mainly for the transport of our own feelings.

Again, Iris Murdoch's well-known fondness for the doubling, if not trebling, of themes and motifs (a truly Shakespearian prolixity here) is a quality which frequently causes readers to confuse wood and trees. To mention her predilection for magic, witchcraft, symbolic names, impenetrable sibling relationships, letters, weather, playacting, bells, roses, dogs, foreigners, concentration camps, and cancer, is to recall not one book but her entire opus, which sometimes seems to be composed of a series of intricate variations upon a handful of themes. When certain effects recur, as the ritual breast-showing does, for instance, in *The Flight From The Enchanter* and *The Italian Girl*, they take on a mythic quality which is quite mesmerising; and to read a new Iris Murdoch in the light of all that she has written before, is akin to the feeling of the acolyte as another layer of the *arcana* is revealed to him.

There can be little doubt that Iris Murdoch quite deliberately sets out to create little puzzles and intellectual teasers for her readers. She expects, for example, that we will be sufficiently well informed to know the Latin meaning of the name of Felix in *An Unofficial Rose* (1962); but is this an ironic reflection upon his bad fortune in having his life broken apart by his beloved Ann and her cruel, killing other half, her daughter Miranda, or does it subtly indicate his luck in *escaping* from them, like the adulterous husband Randall (randy?)? Iris Murdoch persuades us that her own system of cross-referencing is so complex that we are encouraged to supply our own links from literature, history and life; thus, in *Under The Net* (1954), the Fall of Rome is surely an ironic allusion to the failure of an ideal of democracy, as well as a gentle gibe at the Hollywood epic which is such a feature of our modern period. Mischa Fox's name, in *The Flight From The Enchanter* may plausibly be accounted a vernacular evocation of Jonson's Volpone, but is also intended to summon up the actual animal for us, to bring out Mischa's feral attributes.

We could go on like this for hours. Often the significances proliferate more fully and suggestively. In *The Time Of The Angels* Elizabeth is presented as a Lady of Shallott figure (the web

THE FICTION OF SEX

image is operative in this context), while otherwise she is a white form opposing the Black Madonna of the coloured servant Pattie in the structure of the novel. Pattie's door-keeping function also makes her a kind of Cerberus, so that by extension the Rectory which she guards so devotedly is Hell. Along this line the dreadful Muriel is an angel of death (this links with her destructiveness as a false writer, committed to the death of truth); and Marcus's entry through the black coal hole and up the "back passage" makes him inescapably demonic—or is it simply a comic metaphor for his repressed homosexuality? The beauty of this writer is that we can play these games of association and still all be right—or all wrong, and it will not matter.

But this concentration upon the White Witch of Oxford can obscure the sly social satirist at work. It has been fashionable to bring out the purely imaginative elements of Iris Murdoch's writing, the magic, the myth, the religions primitive and modern, the old dark gods of convention and the new dark gods of neurosis. At times it seems as if the reader has to be permanently at the full stretch of his interpretative capacity in order not to miss a jot or tittle of the philosophy, metaphysics, and general enchantment which she hands out. What is equally important is the vein of naturalism, typically observed and recorded straight from life in minute social detail. It is arguable that later ages may come to regard her work somewhat in the way that we now look at Dickens, as an historian and reporter of his epoch as much as an inspired teller of tall tales. Earlier in her career, some of the social observation is not as sharp as it later becomes. In *The Sandcastle* (1957), for instance, it is never made plain how Mor, the minor public schoolmaster and close friend of the Churchillian Demoyte, can simply expect to pick up a safe Labour parliamentary seat, even granted that his friend Tim is Chairman of the Constituency Labour Party, and that these are the palmy days of the nineteen-fifties before Socialism became modish. There is, too, always the threat of the flicker of patrician disdain, if not the sneer at least the raised eyebrow, at the sauce bottles on the sideboard, the overcareful vowels, the flushed face and the bulging thigh.

Yet over the years there is an increasing mastery of command over this type of material. Iris Murdoch has clearly given some thought and effort to polishing up this aspect of her not inconsiderable repertoire of effects: her most recent triumph in this genre is *An Accidental Man* (1971), which, with its large cast of juveniles and socialites, its comment upon the student problem, the state of the economy, and the Vietnam war, must claim to be among the most comprehensive of current social satires. There is even a moment when Austin, the central character, muses comfortably, "What was so relaxing about Mitzi was that he did not care a fuck what Mitzi thought". This use of the obscenity not in a challenging but in a totally casual context, places the work in the period after the great battles concerning such usage in literature and society have been fought and won—or lost, depending on your viewpoint. In this and many other small ways the novel is so precisely of its time that it conveys the very flavour of the year in which it was written.

Yet even at its most pointed Iris Murdoch's satire is not marked by the contemptuous detachment, nor the quivering irresistible urge to "flap the bug with gilded wings" which we associate with our classical satirists. Hers is truly the blend of laughter and love which Dostoevsky so acutely isolated. If we can pick up one thread more than any other from the dense fabric of her fictions, we can single out this; the importance of love, the scarcity of it, and the desperate difficulty, if not impossibility, of even approximating to its rigorous demands. Most of the characters have to settle for far less than full happiness: they have to take what they can get and console themselves with that; they have to agree with the summary of *An Accidental Man* that "love, even fake love, even dream love, was something after all".

"Fake love, dream love"; Iris Murdoch is especially interested in the people living in frameworks socially sanctioned as the vehicle of love, which may in fact cover up its absence or deny its existence. Love is conventionally understood as expressed in and through marriage, but it is Iris Murdoch's somewhat gnomic utterance in *The Sandcastle* that "a married couple is a dangerous machine". *The Bell, An Unofficial Rose, Bruno's Dream, The Black Prince*, and others of her novels give us marriages in states of decay of dissolution. More painful perhaps is the study of the marriage in which both partners are still very much alive and

147

kicking, in which the power of the institution, as a terrible mechanism *sui generis*, is laid bare with an appalling clarity. Has the day-to-day misery of living in an unequal partnership often been described as well as this?

> He suffered deeply from the discovery that his wife was the stronger. He told himself that her strength sprang only from obstinate and merciless unreason; but to think this did not save him either from suffering coercion or from feeling resentment. He could not now make his knowledge of her into love, he could not even make it into indifference. In the heart of him he was deeply compelled. He was forced. And he was continually offended.
>
> (*The Sandcastle*, pp. 10–11)

Clearly on this view of life, any structured relationship, not only marriage, can be an engine of unforeseen danger and destruction. Iris Murdoch's interest in sinister siblings is so well known as to need no further comment here. Love, understood as the selfless concern for another's welfare above one's own, is more frequently expressed in Iris Murdoch's fiction through unhallowed relationships than through those we are all familiar with; it is as if the extra trials involved in keeping up a feeling which cuts across the barricades of class, age, or sex, will themselves define and continually test the genuineness of it. A classic illustration is to be found in the homosexual marriage between Simon and Axel in *A Fairly Honourable Defeat* (1970). Theirs is a very conventional and discreet union; Axel especially has a fastidious horror of the seedy underworld of London lavatories and young soldiers. Their day-to-day living is also solidly constructed as an echo of a heterosexual marriage—Axel is strong and silent, good at taking decisions and winning bread; Simon is dependent, fearful, extravagant, and convinced he's "not good enough" for Axel, but nevertheless a lovely cook and a sweet person.

Yet although they move in a circle of worldly and tolerant people and are not forced into ignominious antics to conceal their love, they are still under constant pressure from the hostility or incomprehension of certain people, and from the doubts and fears within themselves that their "marriage" can survive. It is a reversal of all our carefully-created expectations when the relationship between these two men does prove supple and strong enough to withstand the assaults on it of private malice and public ignorance. It is also highly ironic that at the end of this novel, a story very much about marriage in modern times, the sun goes down upon two un-marriages, two partnerships between a pair of homosexuals and a pair of sisters.

Iris Murdoch does not exclude the possibility of sexual expression of feeling in such relationships as these. But in the main she is concerned to establish that there is no such thing as an intrinsic connection between love and sex, indeed she tries hard to resist and to undermine in her work the contemporary confusing of the two. This conviction, that these are *not* the same, nor even necessarily kin, is a vital principle of her fiction (it is also a central theme of her husband John Bayley's book, *The Characters of Love*). See how many times Iris Murdoch casts an eye of the sort that is commonly described as unerring over the laboured contortions of the human frame caught in the act of (may we meaningfully say?) love:

> A projection upon one body is laboriously inserted into a hole in another . . . a pitiful awkward ugly inefficient piece of fleshy mechanism. . . . It's supposed to be something to do with love, at least that's the legend, but love is just a comforting myth and even if it wasn't it couldn't possibly have any connection with sex. We don't mix up love with eating do we? Or with farting or hiccuping or blowing one's nose? Or with breathing? Or with the circulation of the blood or the operation of the liver? Then why connect it with our curious impulse to shove parts of ourselves inside other people, or with our in some ways equally curious impulse to thrust our damp evil-smelling mouths and decaying teeth up against other such unsavoury gluey orifices in other bodies? Answer me that, dear lady.
>
> (*A Fairly Honourable Defeat*, Chapter Five)

This emphasis upon the absurdity of sexual behaviour originates partly in Iris Murdoch's belief that it is, or should be, an entirely personal activity, yet it so rarely is. A married couple may or may not be a dangerous machine; but whatever else it is a mechanism peculiar to itself, a bicycle made for two, and the knowledge or observation of a third party invariably allows the dimension of the absurd to creep in. Thus Isobel's comically

Puritan disdain of sex activity which Iris Murdoch herself links with that expression of animal vitality which she admires so much: "I've heard them whining and barking at each other." This reaction is juxtaposed with her husband's more admiring response to variations on the theme: "I read in a paper about a man who couldn't make love to his wife unless he had her all tied up in brown paper like a parcel" (*The Italian Girl*). Partly, too, sex may be absurd because the body itself is so. There is at times in the minds of Iris Murdoch's characters a whiff of Augustinian despair and disgust at the exigencies of the flesh, even a sense of *soma sema*, the body is the tomb. Here Mitzi, a gross Amazon and one of those grotesques of Iris Murdoch who are intensely real to themselves if to no-one else, muses upon the men in her life:

> The sky was producing rain again. Austin said, "I'll go and pee if you don't mind". He went through the studio and out into the ragged garden. Mitzi followed and watched him. He went over by the wall with his back to her. As the sky slowly darkened he looked like Mr Secombe-Hughes, standing there sturdily with his feet apart. The smell of male urine was wafted on the damp air. I hate men, she thought. I just hate men. I hate them.
>
> (*An Accidental Man*, p. 29)

How strange it all is, and how hard! The wonder in the Iris Murdoch universe is that love can exist at all, menaced as it is on every side. We are all frail; and even relatively trivial things like the weather, emotional upsets, alcohol, can dislocate our responses and distract our attention from the other person and the business of loving in hand. A philosophical statement of this point occurs in an earlier essay (*The Yale Review*, vol. 49, Winter 1960): "I take the general consciousness today to be ridden either by convention or by neurosis"; these are "the enemies of understanding, one might say the enemies of love". Iris Murdoch amplified this in *The Sovereignty Of Good*, 1970, p. 91, in a way that throws considerable light upon her own concept and process of character development:

> The difficulty is to keep the attention fixed upon the real situation and to prevent it from returning surreptitiously to the self with consolations of self-pity, resentment, fantasy, and despair. The

refusal to attend may even induce a fictitious sense of freedom: I may as well toss a coin . . . it is a *task* to come to see the world as it is.

So in various ways we lose touch and fail. Iris Murdoch sums it up, "In the moral life the enemy is the fat relentless ego" (*The Sovereignty Of Good*, p. 52). Loving is the most basic of moral activities in life; and the task which Iris Murdoch enjoins upon her characters and by implication upon her readers too, that of maintaining "respect for the real", is probably the most immediate form of loving that most of us are required to undertake. Human failure and its attendant compensatory actions frequently mean though that love, far from restoring and re-creating, becomes a form of assault; and few writers have given more attention than Iris Murdoch to its power of destruction. Love as rape, love as enslavement, love the prerogative and stock-in-trade of the manipulator, the entangler, the false prophet— how these few phrases delineate the outlines of the Murdoch landscape and conjure up that race of character-types she has made her own! All her readers must have their favourite example of the species—Palmer in *A Severed Head*, Matthew in *An Accidental Man*, Mischa in *The Flight From The Enchanter*, Julius in *A Fairly Honourable Defeat*, Arnold in *The Black Prince*. Each of these, in his respective narrative framework, is an active enemy of truth and love; each joins with all the other inert forces and impediments to understanding and fidelity in the attempt to render lifeless a relationship in his vicinity. This activity, though in Iris Murdoch's fiction as in real life it commonly goes unreprehended and even undetected, is felt to be, quite simply, an offence of the first order. It is a primal outrage, because a moral one.

Most people today, in the West at least, do not go to war. They need not even know that it occurs elsewhere unless they choose to. They do not engage much in politics, even at a local level; they do not commit thievery and murder; they do not, obviously at least, go mad. But they do have to live out and work through personal lives in which the boss, the wife, the first husband, the teenage offspring, the elderly relative, offer their mite of trouble and demand some response, if not solution. If Iris Murdoch only offered us some description and analysis of these life situations, that would be good enough. But she gives us too a moral frame, a series of standards by which we may judge not only the characters in her fictions but the characters of life itself. In this lies the importance and relevance of her contribution to the twentieth-century novel and in an era where the moral stance has increasingly been abandoned in favour of the psychological probe, Iris Murdoch's fusion of the two makes hers a unique voice.

6

The "Liberation"

Impossible to avoid the conclusion. A few of the women were writing in no way women had ever written before. . . . It was a good style. At its best it read with the tension of an anger profound enough to be kept under the skin. Every point was made with a minimum of words, a mean style, no question of that. It used obscenity with the same comfort a whore would take with her towel.

(Norman Mailer, *The Prisoner of Sex*, 1971, pp. 39–40)

Men, some to business, some to pleasure take;
But every woman is at heart a rake.
(Alexander Pope, *Moral Essays*, Epistle Two,
To a Lady)

Our age has seen a fracturing of literary, social, and personal taboos which amounts in short to a reassessment of the obscene. Previous constraints upon naturalistic treatment of sexual and excremental functions have been eroded to an unprecedented extent. This has inevitably brought with it certain problems, not least that of public response. As Havelock Ellis was concerned to stress in *The Revaluation Of Obscenity* (1931), p. 5, "the taboo on the excremental obscene is only conventional and social, while that on the sexual obscene is regarded as also moral and religious". We might add political too; the efforts of many women to redefine their sexual natures is explicitly linked with the examination of women's place in society at large, with a reconsideration of the female role in literature and life. From the late nineteen-fifties in England, in the last ten or fifteen years at most, a distinctive feature of modern fiction has been the abandoning of the nineteenth-century concept of a female's duty to maintain moral standards in society through her position in the family ("The Angel At The Hearth"). Women have been relinquishing the unsatisfying and often delusory "sphere of influence" for that of direct involvement in action, especially sexual action. Any such effort is the natural opposite of that delicacy which has for so long been a prerequisite of femininity. We are witnessing the emergence of a new type of woman, or a new version of what Hardy called "the ache of modernity".

This newness does not lie wholly in the flexing of muscles not fully used before. Tough cookies, *per se*, are nothing new; we need think no further back than Charlotte Brontë's real-life and fictional definitions of woman's lot, or of Jane Austen's Elinor Dashwood or Anne Elliot, while even in Dickens, the Daddy of Daddies, there are many examples of women who endure and who survive. This is also true on a lower contemporary level; the two central female characters in Mrs Henry Wood's sensationally successful *East Lynne* (1861) are both strong and capable in their different ways. The best of the nineteenth-century literary heroines were never housebound and vapourish. But the Victorian imagination in general was curiously attracted to the ideal of the woman who expressed through her own weakness an overblown tribute to the man's strength and competence—this in part accounts for the contemporary masculine fascination with "green fruit", the unpleasing underbelly of the Victorian protective exaltation of the undeveloped female. And the independence of the heroines of the fiction of this time, however real in the short term, usually assumes a return to the shelter of the man's cloak and comfort when it can be found and achieved—note the touching abandoned child, wandering orphan, and lost bird or little animal imagery which so frequently accompanies nineteenth-century fictional descriptions of women alone. Where the woman had to continue in her solitary state, this was frequently shown to be a punishment for some error or failing; the man's protection, the domestic reward, have been lost through female fault. In diametric contrast some modern women do not regard freedom from the ties of hearth and home as the punishment, but the prize. They seek independence, and wish to retain it.

This desire, often expressed with uncompromising directness, has naturally provoked some opposition and resentment. Mailer describes the devastating effect of the new women's writing upon men readers—"A wind in this prose whistled up the skirts of male conceit. The basis of male conceit was that men could live with truths too unsentimental for women to support (hence the male mind was gifted with superior muscles just so much as the back)." Mary Ellman, in *Thinking About Women*, also stresses the significance in literature of the new independence of women. As more and more are making their way out of the doll's house, she observes that "the old animal drama of male pursuit does not hold. Instead now, women tend to offer and men to refuse—or to be incapable of accepting, or to regret having accepted". This may in fact merely mean that the old cave-man fantasy of brute physical domination is being replaced by a subtler form of mastery and punishment, in the parental mode, of withdrawal of love, withholding of approval; and the male in many literary relationships remains the unquestioned arbiter.

However, we are not perhaps really talking about new content of behaviour, but new expressions in form. It is doubtful that any age can really develop a new type, yet it remains the illusion of various generations that they are evolving new problems, new characters, new advances in emotional technology. The critic Jean Gagen has described a New Woman in Elizabethan and Jacobean drama in his book of that name; and more recently both Hardy and Ibsen in their quite different ways have been accused of giving birth to New Women. But in our time the novel really has lived up to its name—women's new social freedoms, their adventures, mental, and especially physical, have provided totally novel material for writers. Doris Lessing acknowledges in herself "whole areas of me made by the kind of experience women haven't had before", and shows a strong sense of her characters being a different breed. Her women are "on some kind of frontier", and know it; see her ironic labelling of her heroines as "free women" throughout *The Golden Notebook*.

Such revaluations are not accomplished without disturbance. If the contemporary version of the New Woman is not popular with men, she is not especially fond of herself either. Quite frequently, in her efforts to be "free", the woman detaches herself from her existing support, be it family, husband, or work, and finds that she is ill-equipped to face the troubling wastes of a solitary existence. The price she pays for her "freedom" is counted in loss and desolation. There have of course been earlier delineations of the psycho-neurotic heroine; Fanny in *Mansfield Park* is a touching study of how it feels to be nervous and sad, and Gwendolen, in *Daniel Deronda* (1876), nursing her "heart-sores", faces a life "without pleasure or hope of pleasure" after her marriage to Grandcourt (Book V, Chapter XXXV). But recent women's fiction, in its search for the source and location of female identity, in its contingent consideration of female weakness and strength, may seem to display an undue concentration upon debility and neurosis.

Today's heroine of fiction is all too frequently a paralysed, suffering, inadequate creature. To those who prefer their women simpler and straighter, the new woman is a gloomy soul. In fulfilling the twentieth-century fictional imperative to go inward, many writers have created characters who suggest that they cannot bear it when they get in there. To others, she presents a realistic picture of a modern woman caught in the trap between realism and romance, painfully unlearning the lessons of adolescence, absorbed just as much from *Jane Eyre* as from *Woman's Own*—for dark and fascinating men tend not to appear too often over the typewriter, the shop counter, or the washing machine, and all too soon the female horizon is bounded by Superbore or Superbastard rather than by Superman. Margaret Drabble has described criticism of her concentration on the daily realities of life as depressing, her alliance with what she humorously calls "the 'nose-in-the-washing-machine' school of fiction". In fairness to Margaret Drabble, most of her characters seem to work up and away from it; her heroines do throw off the domestic trammels in favour of some version of personal freedom, however superficially defined. We may wonder, though, how far this process simply represents a conventional provision of a happy ending for the heroine. What genuine hope or conviction is Rose left with at the end of *The Needle's Eye*, for instance?

It is at the least arguable that the social and personal freedoms obtained in this century have in fact undermined or enfeebled some women. Writers as different as Jennifer Dawson in *The Ha-Ha* (1961), and Sylvia Plath in *The Bell Jar* (1963) have dealt memorably with the theme of alienation and mental distress. Perhaps better known of those who have numbered and inspected the pieces as they drop off the crumbling female ego is Penelope Mortimer. Her heroine of *The Pumpkin Eater* (1962) has little autonomy from the first—a bewildered girlhood is succeeded by a badgered wifehood in which everybody else has more edge and conviction, more drive and purpose, than she has. She is overborne by her father's "pipe down" when she objects to her three eldest children being sent off to boarding school; the motive here is woman-excluding masculine solidarity—"I'm not going to have you crushing the boy with responsibility from the word go". The father hopes that the fourth husband Jake will succeed with the woman where he has failed—"It's time she had a firm hand on her tiller" (note the parody of strong masculine jargon, with its implied innuendo, nudge and wink).

It is the centre of the heroine's problem of living that she can express none of the resentment she feels: "I burned with anger, but dully." In a final spasm of submission she consents to a termination of pregnancy followed by a sterilisation, only to be confronted by the unbearable irony of her husband's mistress's pregnancy; an irony compounded by the suggestion (of the mistress's husband) that the girl would have finished with Jake had his wife's pregnancy continued. The final submission is to the husband's values and terms of living, which in his definition is "necessarily defective, vicious, careless, an inevitable time of activity between two deaths". After crisis, illness, flight, and retreat, the heroine reflects, "I was no longer frightened of him. I accepted him at last, because he was inevitable". This conclusion might seem to run the risk of alienating both women and men, indeed anyone disinclined to swallow this low-key assessment of marriage expectations—even the charmless Jake, with his mindless egotism and his reflex philandering, deserves, one feels, to be more than "inevitable".

The point, though, is not whether or not we like Penelope Mortimer's heroine (who, incidentally, is still weaving her sorrowful way through *The Home*, 1971). It is incontrovertibly a new direction for fiction at large, and for women's writing in particular, that it should render in such close and immediate terms the sensations of the castaway. But important as this development has been, it has been overshadowed by the use of modern fiction to reveal and examine the bodily rather than the mental processes of twentieth-century womankind. There has been remarkably little interest in political emancipation; the recent wave of feminism has washed over most novelists, and "Women's Lib." has been left to the dramatists and the polemicists (see David Hare's *Slag*, and the essays of Kate Millett, Germaine Greer, Juliet Mitchell, and Sheila Rowbotham as approaches to this subject). Novelists have made the most of the recently-acquired prerogative to mention the unmentionable; and as the narcissism of the female artist has for so long been denied this outlet, it is perhaps not surprising that it has burst out with some force.

Not that the subject has been unthought of by former women writers. That essentially chastest of novelists, Virginia Woolf, in a description of her own early career, adverted to the forbidden theme in these words:

> The image that comes to my mind when I think of this girl is the image of a fisherman lying sunk in dreams on the verge of a deep lake with a rod held out over the water. She was letting her imagination sweep unchecked round every rock and cranny of the world that lies submerged in the depths of our unconscious being. Now came the experience, the experience that I believe to be far commoner with women writers than with men. The line raced through the girl's fingers. Her imagination had rushed away. It had sought the pools, the depths, the dark places where the largest fish slumber. And then there was a smash. There was an explosion. There was foam and confusion. The imagination had dashed itself against something hard. The girl was roused from her dream. She was indeed in a state of the most acute and difficult distress. To speak without figure she had thought of something, something about the body, about the passions which it was unfitting for her as a woman to say. Men, her reason told her, would be shocked. The consciousness of what men will say of a woman who speaks the truth about her passions had roused her from her artist's state of unconsciousness. She could write no more. The trance was over. Her imagination could work no longer. This I believe to be a very common experience with women writers—they are impeded by the extreme conventionality of the other sex. For though men sensibly allow themselves great freedom in these respects, I doubt that they realise or can control the extreme severity with which they condemn such freedom in women.

Reflecting on this, Virginia Woolf concludes, "telling the truth about my own experiences as a body, I do not think I solved. I doubt that any woman has solved it yet. The obstacles against her are still immensely powerful—and yet they are very difficult to define. Outwardly, what is simpler than to write books? Outwardly, what obstacles are there for a woman rather than for a man? Inwardly, I think, the case is very different; she has still many ghosts to fight, many prejudices to overcome" ("Professions For Women", *The Death Of The Moth*, pp. 152–3).

Note the assumption that it would take time, but only time, for the inner censor to be winkled out and sent packing. So it has proved. For the first time in the history of fiction women have been describing their experiences as sexual beings. For the first time they are challenging the long-undisturbed masculine versions of such events, whether that of "Fanny Hill", Frank Harris, D. H. Lawrence, or John Updike. Candid treatment of sexual topics is as old as man's sense of himself. What is new is that first, women are describing in detail and widely publishing descriptions of sexual activity seen from the woman's point of view; and second, that they are committing to print accounts of the specifically female areas of sensuality and sexuality which have hitherto been neglected, childbirth, menstruation, masturbation, and lesbianism. Few passages so clearly illustrate the historical movement towards more and more exposure of body and of sensations than this characteristically febrile extract from Rosamond Lehmann's *The Weather in the Streets* (1936):

> Then it was afterwards. He said, whispering:
> "I'm your lover. . . ."
> I thought about it. I had a lover. But nothing seemed changed. It wasn't disappointing exactly. . . . The word is: unmomentous. . . . Not wonderful—yet. . . . I couldn't quite look at him, but it was friendly and smiling. His cheek looked coarse-grained in the light of the lamp. I saw the hairs in his nostrils. . . .
>
> (1968 edition, p. 153)

In the context of this reticence, even the grain of Rollo's cheek and the hairs of his nose assume the status of startling and abrasive physical detail; but readers who agree with Virginia Woolf that "stories that follow people into their private rooms are difficult" will be grateful that the writer takes us no further.

Virginia Woolf backs up this reference in *The Waves* with one of those sequences, relatively rare in her work, in which she allowed her gift of irony full play. Her description of the efforts of Bernard to take the other boys into the private room of Dr Crane, the headmaster, has the quality almost of prophetic warning as she parodies the dangers of the revelatory style, the groping for the appropriately suggestive detail, the grandiose fantasy, and the striking of attitudes, which are its common features:

> The two rooms are united by a bridge of rosy light from the lamp at the bedside where Mrs Crane lies with her hair on the pillow reading a French memoir. As she reads, she sweeps her hand with an abandoned and despairing gesture over her forehead, and sighs, "Is this all?" comparing herself with some French duchess.
>
> (p. 36)

Again seen in its comic aspect, sexual intercourse is not infrequently presented by Virginia Woolf as a coarse or low-class activity—"the growl of the bootboy making love to the tweeny among the gooseberry bushes". Does she intend in the last phrase here a joking reference to the time-honoured formula for evading sexual description? It is at the least a linguistic felicity, one would think.

This is, however, as far as she goes, and in her time even a masculine growl could be considered rather near the knuckle in polite fiction. By 1963, the defloration of Dottie, conducted amid the echoing shades of Kraft-Ebbing, *A Midsummer Night's Dream*, and her lover's memories of previous lovers, occupies a full chapter of *The Group*. Mary McCarthy ironically relates every detail of tumescence and detumescence, and is sufficiently detached from her material to insist on its unromantic and even absurd aspects; the lover goes to sleep immediately on completion of the intercourse, while Dottie is left wondering what's happening; and when he propels her from his door with the command, "Get yourself a pessary", she thinks he is urging on her a peccary. Despite these unpromising circumstances, she has the surprise of her sheltered life with him. Orgasm succeeds orgasm as Dottie throws off the girlhood conditioning and restraints of social class (the lover nicknames her "Boston") along with her clothes. Although the McCarthy irony is everywhere present, Dottie's feelings of adventure, excitement, pleasure, and eventually triumph, are faithfully recorded. We are asked to accept that in its modest way Dottie's *is* something of a triumph; here is a new type, the timid female freebooter embarked on the high seas of sexual discovery.

Mary McCarthy has been widely censured for her critical method of novel-writing, which to some resembles the transfixing of the live butterfly for display; and Dottie may also be seen as one among many in the showcase of female folly which *The Group* offers its readers. But if we are to have fictional representations of women's sexuality, how much preferable is the astringent to the pseudo-poetic. The modern mistress of this vein is Edna O'Brien, whose lush and overblown prose has commanded more than its due share of admirers. Here she is offering the tribute of her pen to her heroine's one-night-stand with a man dimly remembered from a long-ago party who has stopped by, just temporarily, to take a break from his wife, his four children, his mistress, and his problems:

> Relief. She thought, he means to stay until morning, and that pleased her as much as that he was going to sleep with her. She remembered a man who got up and left after he came, while she was still in the throes of desire.
>
> In bed she opened wide. And christened him foxglove because it too grew high and purple in a dark secretive glade. He put the bedside light on. She felt him harden and lengthen inside her like a stalk. Soft and hard together. He loved her as no man had ever done, not even the husband who first sundered her and started off the whole cycle of longing and loving and pain and regret. Because that kind of love is finally emptying.
>
> "You loved me lovely," she said. His back was bathed in sweat. He had laboured on her behalf and she was filled with the most inordinate gratitude.
>
> (*August Is A Wicked Month*, 1965, Chapter Two)

Not the stuff of which sexual adventuresses are made, one might think. But this is to underrate the manifold resorts of the heroine's inertia and passivity. A new experience comes her way when she is unable to resist the demands made by another casual lover that he should immortalise the moment on celluloid:

> He crossed over and drew down one strap of her dress so that it fell on her arm. The white sagging top of one breast came

into view. Above it was a line of raw pink where she had boiled in the sun that morning in an effort to get a tan for him. He photographed her like that and then with both straps down so that the sag of both breasts was in view and then he brought her dress down round her waist and photographed her naked top. It had been too hot to put on a brassière. From his position, stooped behind the camera, he indicated that she hold one breast, perkily, as if she enjoyed showing it off.

(Chapter Seven)

This, clearly, is an example of what Doris Lessing had in mind when she referred to "the sort of experience women haven't had before" (lady-novelist women, that is). Part at least of Edna O'Brien's stylistic difficulty must be located in the novelty of her material—there simply are no precedents or traditions for this kind of writing. If an author chooses to do without the deflationary safeguard of humour in the treatment of sexual matters, in the way that Mary McCarthy uses it, for example, then the discovery of the appropriate tone and vocabulary presents enormous problems.

Edna O'Brien made another effort to find a method adapted to this material in the experimental *A Pagan Place* (1970). This novel attempts to give a child's-eye view of sexual experience, both its own and that of the adults around it. When we know that it is set in Ireland (where else?) we are alerted to expect the usual Celtic quota of torment and twilight; and we are not disappointed. Here, in these desperately impoverished and limited surroundings, the only diversions lie in watching the village idiot and listening to visitors using the lavatory; and a child is brought up among "things to fear from the living and from the dead". Sexual exploration is the child's only entertainment. In order to draw the reader into the young girl's experience, perhaps also to recreate the freshness and immediacy of the original occasion, Edna O'Brien uses throughout her narrative the unusual second-person device, and this combines with the equally esoteric nature of the material to produce some strange effects. What, one wonders, does Harold Pinter, the book's dedicatee, make of a line like this: "You sat and put a doll's big soft toe between your legs outside your knickers, and tickled yourself"? Again, readers who find this sort of approach pawky and distasteful will be further repelled by the sub-Joycean references to "snot" and so on, and the pervasive use of infantile slang, "diddies", "number two", "do pooly", for instance.

Whimsy like this is a more specialised taste than humour, and Edna O'Brien is on firmer ground when presenting her schoolteacher, the "brainy" Miss Davitt, who opines that "toothpaste was probably of Greek origin, like all civilised things". When cross with her pupils she sets them to write on "A Day In The Life Of A Penny". There is much incidental pleasure, too, in some characteristically Irish witticisms and absurdities. One situation is laconically summed up in the observation that "Hell hath no music like a woman playing second fiddle". What Ivy Compton-Burnett calls "the fine edge of family life" is also brought out by the use of humour. The youngest daughter is engrossed in First Love: "You sent him a letter in secret. You wrote Remembrance is all I ask, but if remembrance should prove a task, Forget me. It seemed a bit extreme once you had posted it." Meanwhile, the elder and unmarried daughter's pregnancy has brought the doctor to condole with the father, who is reeling under the far more serious affliction of the death of the mare; and the doctor is understandably disturbed by the father's lamentation that "her flesh was sold in France as a delicacy". Finally, humour is significantly used in the presentation of the key sexual sequence, where the young girl is given her introduction to men by a young priest who is "very partial to Mary Magdalene". The girl is overwhelmed—"It was an honour"—and in imagination clothes him in his vestments and cassock to sustain and intensify the effect. The climax is rendered with a refined sense of the ridiculous: "Never had the corneas of eyes bulged so."

There is a weakness, however, in the intermittent nature of the use of humour. Most of the young girl's feelings and observations about sex are set down with a leaden solemnity, as if sacrosanct. The child's development pales, too, in comparison with the interest of her mother. This characterisation is the true heart and real strength of the book. It contains both the power of generalisation and the acute particularity of fine writing; it could stand for any Irish mother and yet is very evidently a portrait of a woman locked in a precise situation. We see her domestic desperation, harassed by money worries and a pig of a husband, whose joyless sexual attentions are yet another anxiety to her rather than a source of any warmth or comfort. Her primitive efforts at contraception, using the tissue from shoe-boxes, are vividly recalled by the child: "Before she went across the landing she put tissue paper in the inside of her pussy . . . over there she moaned and groaned. His sinews crackled." Her life is shadowed by the need to "manage" her bad-tempered and unreliable husband, and she shows a degraded facility in various servile ruses and placatory devices to obviate his going off on drunken binges. Later there is a poignant episode when she goes to the big city in search of a runaway daughter; we see her frantically scouring the streets but pathetically bewildered by urban life and unable even to use the telephone. The novel closes with her, locked in her room, howling with grief as her youngest child leaves home for the convent.

Few children, however well drawn, could hold our interest in competition with a character of this strength, especially when the author so perversely restricts herself to the limiting terms and repetitive rhythms of childhood speech: "Often she slighted you and said you were trash and said Be off, trash." It seems clear that Edna O'Brien expects the reader to accept that there is a built-in sanctity and fascination in a child's response to life. This may be seen not only from her own uncritical attitude to the childhood material in the book, but also from her pronouncement that "an artist and a child and a madman have some similar components". Readers who find that they can have too much even of a good thing are advised to take cover; in the same interview Edna O'Brien informed her public, "I've a great amount of childhood still in me" (*T.V. Times*, January 1973).

On the other hand, though, the concentration upon this theme does at least reduce the amount of print expended upon sexual intercourse, which children, even today, tend to have less often than adults. There are many people now who feel that they have had enough of sex as a topic. For it is not as if one woman writer writes for all, so that one description of a fine and private female moment will do for everyone. On the contrary, each woman writer is not only impelled to work out her own version of the "and then he . . ." story, but in certain cases will return again and again to the topic, as her experience, and the mind of the public, is broadened.

Some process of this sort is at work with Doris Lessing, whose career aptly illustrates the "liberation" we are talking about. In early versions of the bedroom scene, she was forced by the then prevailing conventions into the use of the "and then it was afterwards" formula. The autobiographical novel *Martha Quest* pushes as hard as it could in its time against the boundaries of the convention—the man is described as undressing, down to the unromantic detail of his removing his shoes and placing them neatly together before getting on to the bed. There is even reference to a condom (chastely described as "a packet"). But the main course of the action is conducted within the safety of the romantic generalisation, and the abstract or Latin term: "the act"; "the forms of sensitive experience", "a drenching, saturating moment of illumination". Not unnaturally the lover fails to provide this, but the heroine reflects on the hope of better luck next time: "and afterwards she lay coiled meekly beside him like a woman in love, for her mind had swallowed the moment of disappointment whole, like a python. . . ."

Much had changed by the time Doris Lessing came to publish *The Golden Notebook* in 1962; and much was changed as a result of this often very brave book. Doris Lessing is unflinching in her confrontation of the discrepancy between reality and romance in most women's lives, and especially in their sexual experience. One aspect of female behaviour which she illustrates more thoroughly than any other woman writer of our time, is the ease with which a sexual failure or disappointment becomes a pattern of perseverating unsuccess. Eventually, even, the woman is driven to seek only those encounters which will fulfil her worst expectations. This is how one of the Lessing heroines (all four of whom may plausibly be seen as different aspects of the same female nature) approaches intercourse with a man who does not attract her. Ella (elle?) works herself up to it by thinking that a man goes to bed without scruples, and so should she be able to. Thus fortified, she is able to bring out "Would you like to go to bed with me?" After this venture into masculine assertiveness she then relapses into little servant girl: "Well, now, *sir*, I think you should set me at my ease, or something." He tries, but it is a loveless encounter:

> In bed, it was a delightful shock of warm tense flesh. (Ella was standing to one side, thinking ironically; Well, well!) He pene-

trated her almost at once, and came after a few seconds. She was about to console or be tactful, when he rolled on his back, flung up his arms, and exclaimed: "Boy. Oh boy!"

(At this point Ella became herself, one person, both of them thinking at one). She lay beside him, controlling physical disappointment, smiling.

(p. 277)

All Doris Lessing's heroines are afflicted with this service philosophy in their view of their own sex. They fear to make demands of men, even those of common humanity, in case any show of eagerness should frighten them off and nip the unfolding "romance" in the bud. Taken to extremes, this becomes a kind of masochism; Ella, here, in addition to bearing her own sexual frustrations without reproach, schools herself to lie beside the overhasty lover as he sentimentalises about his wonderful wife and five kids. Even in longer-term relationships, Ella feels no confidence, no security. She senses herself as entirely at the man's mercy for sexual satisfaction, and believes that the quality of her response must depend upon how much the man loves her at that moment.

For in defiance of modern biological discovery, Doris Lessing clings to the old notion of there being two types of orgasm in female sexual response, the vaginal and the clitoral. Rather engagingly, she uses these terms in a highly idiosyncratic way, to differentiate the *emotional* stages of her heroine's love affairs. The vaginal orgasm is a sign to Ella that she really loves Paul— "she could not have experienced it if she had not loved him. It is the orgasm that is created by the man's need for a woman, and his confidence in that need". Again, in her relationship with Michael (it must be coincidental that these unadmirable males are named after saints), Ella is from the first dependent upon his attitude to her and his self-image for her orgasm. She cannot experience it if Michael is moody, withdrawn, or temporarily low in self-esteem. Later, as her love affair with Paul continues but fails to consolidate itself, he expresses the quality of his feeling for Ella by withholding from her her orgasm. He is afraid of committing himself to her by releasing the "emotion" that she sees it as: "A vaginal orgasm is emotion and nothing else . . . the vaginal orgasm is a dissolving in a vague, dark, generalised sensation like

166

being swirled in a warm whirlpool . . . there is only one real female orgasm and that is when a man, from the whole of his need and desire takes a woman and wants all her response" (p. 186).

This is of course the ultimate expression of female dependence and submission. What we have here is the creation of a super-orgasm which can only be achieved in order to satisfy the *man's* need, and in order to make it a fulfilling experience for *him*. The hysteria and uncertainty of the style betray the writer's uneasy sense that she may be out on a limb with this one. The prose is full of hocus-pocus, in which some portentous words and images ("emotion", "dark", "sensation", "a warm whirlpool" —though note the telltale "vague" and "generalised") jostle furtively with the language and attitudes of the woman's magazine —"emotion and nothing else", the "one real" moment, and the man with "the whole of his need and desire"—a lighter and more irreverent writer would have perceived (and suppressed) the inadvertent and unfortunate pun in the last phrase. The "clitoral" orgasm is, naturally, presented as inferior in this strenuous contest. It is achieved through "mechanical means"; this phrase alone shows Ella's dissociation from it as part of a love-experience that she sees Paul's hand as a machine. When their love weakens, he "began to rely on manipulating her externally"—again, the terminology suggests a bone-setter at the end of his resources rather than a loved partner. She resents what she feels is his denial of himself; she sees this orgasm as "a substitute and a fake", and it is consistently opposed against the "real" orgasm. When the lover departs, he takes this with him, so that masturbation, the single woman's recourse, is no satisfaction at all but instead a humiliating reminder that the man has left her:

> She put herself to sleep, as always, by thinking of Paul. She had never, since he had left her, been able to achieve a vaginal orgasm; she was able to reach the sharp violence of the exterior orgasm, her hand becoming Paul's hand, mourning as she did so, the loss of her real self. She slept, overstimulated, nervous, exhausted, cheated.
>
> (p. 264)

It is only fair to point out that Doris Lessing makes some

attempt to present a more objective assessment of the female's sex experience than this. At times the respective merits of the two types of orgasm are discussed with chilling detachment—the "clitoral" is "very exciting", a more varied sensation than the "vaginal" and more powerful. But this dualistic notion does not in any degree loosen its hold upon the writer's mind, and hence upon those of her characters. Paul at one stage asserts that "there are eminent physiologists who say women have no basis for vaginal orgasm". But Ella is not to be weaned away from her reliance upon the *idea* of "the real thing", the irrational rejection of objective discussion in favour of "intuition"—"Then they don't know much, do they?" she says.

With these accounts of masturbation, hitherto the most private of private acts, Doris Lessing takes us well and truly into that area of life which we can categorically say has never been extensively treated in literature before; that is, specifically female experiences set down and analysed by serious women writers for the general readership (I exclude from the discussion earlier and often horrific versions in pornographic and other underground literature). It is rare in the history of art that a rich and previously untapped source of controversial material comes to light, and it is hardly surprising that writers of very different kinds have welcomed an opportunity which has not been available before. Indeed, such has been the amount of public interest in female experiences of this sort that some reputations have been founded securely on this which otherwise might seem to be in themselves rather insubstantial.

Of this order is that of Margaret Drabble. Her fame and significance have been treated in a way that is out of proportion both to the quantity and quality of her output. In retrospective assessment of the nineteen-sixties, it may well appear that Margaret Drabble's greatest gift lay in her sense of timing; she was historically fortunate enough to appear on the literary scene as the first English woman to give voice to the delusive promise of college life, followed by the cold douche of matrimony and childbearing. With a wholly idiosyncratic blend of cleverness and ordinariness, she captured the ear both of the girls who had been to college and those who would like to have been—not to mention the men who were getting, at last, an insight into the mentality and homelife of the bluestocking, with the reassurance that she really is like any other female, underneath.

This is not to underestimate Margaret Drabble's real talents as a prosodist. She is an elegant and often witty writer, with a sharp eye and a deftness at placing and pinning down her characters. But she is hardly a great originator in subject-matter, which is how her admirers see her and how her public image has her. The clever girl caught in the toils of the world, the flesh, and the devil appears *passim* in the fiction of the thirties and forties, and indeed anywhere where clever girls have ever taken up their pens to obtain their revenges or to have their heart's ease; we have already mentioned the two Elizabeths, Bowen and Jane Howard, and it would not be going against the grain of her fiction to add Virginia Woolf, too. The trials of unsupported motherhood (many consider Drabble's pregnant, unmarried Ph.D. in *The Millstone* to be her most unusual creation, including the film company who bought the rights to it), and the whole business of coping alone with an unexpected pregnancy had been anticipated in Lynne Reid Banks's *The L-Shaped Room* (1960). Similarly the humiliation, frustration, and sheer backbreaking work involved in the assorted processes of contraception, breast-feeding, and child-rearing, as handled by Margaret Drabble in her novels, especially *The Waterfall* (1969), have all been dealt with more fully, subtly, and wittily by Mary McCarthy in *The Group*. Consider this sequence, on the horrors entailed in the use and management of the Dutch cap:

> When he wanted to revive within himself his tenderness for her, and to make his own heart bleed, there was a string of incidents which he would recall, which never failed to cause him an intolerable barb of painful emotion. The first of these dated from the second week of their marriage, when, after lying in bed waiting for her, he had got out, finally, and gone to look for her. He heard her before he saw her; she was in the living-room of their small Paddington flat, and she was moaning softly and rhythmically to herself. The light was off, and he did not dare to put it on, but he found her, crouched in a corner behind the armchair, her arms round her knees, wearing her smart trousseau night shirt. Spread-before her on the floor was a Durex Dutch cap, an instruction leaflet, and various other accoutrements of contraception. She

THE FICTION OF SEX

was crying because she could not manage them. She was too
narrow, she said, or rather she did not say, for she did not say
such things, but this was what he gathered, from her meaningless
sobs. He tried to console her, saying that he would occupy himself with such things, as he had always done before their marriage,
in their quite adequately exciting courtship, but the sight of her, so
reduced, had struck him to the heart. And it was too late. Their
first child was conceived that week.

(*Jerusalem The Golden*, 1967, p. 155)

Set that against the sister version, as it were, of the Great
Diaphragm Disaster; and note how the use of humour doesn't
diminish, but increases the pathos and our sense of the woman's
difficulty:

Dottie did not mind the pelvic examination or the fitting. Her
bad moment came when she was learning how to insert the pessary
by herself. Though she was usually good with her hands and well
co-ordinated, she felt suddenly unnerved by the scrutiny of the
doctor and the nurse, so exploratory and impersonal, like the doctor's rubber glove. As she was trying to fold the pessary, the
slippery thing, all covered with jelly, jumped out of her grasp
and shot across the room and hit the steriliser. Dottie could
have died. But apparently this was nothing new to the doctor and
the nurse. "Try again, Dorothy," said the doctor calmly, selecting
another diaphragm of the correct size from the drawer. And, as
though to provide a distraction, she went on to give a little lecture
on the history of the pessary, while watching Dottie's struggles
out of the corner of her eye: how a medicated plug had been
known to the Greeks and Jews and Egyptians, how Margaret Sanger
had found the present diaphragm in Holland, how the long fight had
been waged through the courts here. . . .

(*The Group*, Chapter 3)

Like many writers, Margaret Drabble has not been well served
by her admirers. They have puffed her as the prophetess of the
new emancipated womanhood, when she is nothing of the sort.
Her cool, self-assured, often vinegarish heroines have more in
common with Emma Woodhouse than with Germaine Greer.
Their detachment, too, means that there is an oddly distant
tone imposed even on the closest fictional recordings of intimate
events; they forbid us to become engaged with, or even faintly

170

warm about, the events paraded before us. The effect, then, even when the material is sexual in content, is resolutely asexual, even astringent. This applies to episodes as diverse as the seduction scene in *The Garrick Year* (1964) and the childbirth in *The Mill-stone* (1965). Sex without tears, in brief; and without blood and sweat either, for that matter.

This comment is not intended in disparagement of Margaret Drabble's kind of writing. It takes art to reveal all and show nothing; and when we consider what she does not go into, we may well feel glad that she has spared us all the effort. No such reproach could be lodged against Doris Lessing, whose name crops up so repeatedly in this section because she, above all other women writers, has made it her task to offer a guided tour for her reader through all the highways and byways of the business of being female. The reader could be forgiven for thinking that it must be a grim business indeed. It is arguable that among the disturbing and dangerous effects of the new freedom of recent years has been the intensification of women's physical self-disgust. Freedom to deal in print with menstruation, for instance, may appear to have meant only the opportunity to reveal to a breath-less world what a gruesome affliction the female sex has been suffering in silence throughout history. Lessing makes a cal-culatedly brutal attack upon an assortment of literary and cultural prejudices with the exquisitely feminine line "I stuff my vagina with a tampon of cotton wool".

But this off-hand callousness towards what she elsewhere describes as "the wound inside my body which I didn't choose to have" is misleading. Before setting out for the office the narra-tor, Anna, with a rooted though routine "feeling of shame and modesty", hides her day's supply of tampons in the bottom of her handbag, concealing them under her handkerchief. She justifies, for herself and the reader, this departure from her self-imposed standards of honesty and clarity of behaviour:

> . . . I read recently in some review, a man said he would be re-volted by the description of a woman defecating. I resented this; because, of course, what he meant was he would not like to have that romantic image, a woman, made less romantic. But he was right, for all that. . . . I have instantly to suppress distaste . . . I begin to worry: Am I smelling? . . . the faintly dubious, essenti-

ally stale smell of menstrual blood, I hate. And resent. It is a smell
that I feel as strange even to me, an imposition from outside . . .

(p. 291)

The success of Anna's efforts to suppress distaste may be
judged from an incident later on when she has to break off work
to slip away and wash between her legs, even though she has
already done so before she came out. Anna's experience here
undoubtedly represents that fairly common female attitude to
menstruation which is indicated by its vernacular name, "the
curse". Nevertheless, Anna's dislike is extreme, and verges on
the neurotic. Perhaps most damaging is the association with
defecation. But no less depressing is the self-punishing capitula-
tion to the male viewpoint—"he was right"—and the anxiety
about smelling, the compulsion to make herself acceptable by
the artificial standards of the deodorant advertisements. Anna
is not able to connect this process in any way with human reproduction or with her own body, neither of which in any case
seems at all natural and pleasant to her. Hence she greets it as a
foreign thing, a painful external reminder of a reality which she
has rejected. Doris Lessing never makes this connection, seeming
concerned rather to treat this attitude of Anna sympathetically
as the inevitable burden of the thinking woman. But it is hard
for the attentive reader to avoid linking Anna's withdrawal from her
menstruation with her generally debilitated and impoverished
emotional condition in the novel, her artistic block, her nightmares of aridity, and her fears for her survival as a person.

In Doris Lessing's exploration of Anna's life as a woman alone,
there is one potential solution that is never considered, and that
is life without men. It is significant that women writers have
not taken advantage of the recent freedom from constraints upon
sexual themes to advance our acquaintance with female homosexuality, commonly called "lesbianism". They have indeed found
it much easier to deal with male homosexual love than that expressed between members of their own sex. There has been no
breakdown of barriers here; this theme has had its place for many
years, unquestioned and unremarked, in the pages of some of
our most austere and respected women writers. Typical is the
portrait of the outrageous Julian in Ivy Compton-Burnett's
Brothers and Sisters (1950). It is he, rather than the sister he lives

172

with, who does the flowers and the catering, presides at tea-parties, and constantly invites attention to his delicate sensibilities; he sums it up himself in the sly comment, "Every little womanly touch in this cottage is mine". He adores gossip, and revels in scandal, but on the credit side is quite without pomposity or pretensions to authority, and as a result is an extremely useful agent of the author in contrasting with and puncturing the attitudes of more orthodox male figures, like the clergyman, for instance.

Nevertheless, this is very much an exterior study, embodying some dated clichés of belief, such as that male homosexuals are inevitably effeminate. The same robust and denigratory view is expressed by Enid Bagnold in her presentation of Lewis Afric in *The Loved And The Envied* (1951). This character, whose real name (Snosvic) and nationality (Armenian) are chalked up against him as two black marks from the start, is pointedly made a woman's dress designer in the world of Paris fashion. In case the slow reader should fail to pick up this clue, he is later castigated in round terms as a "pederast", a "pansy", and "one of those unhappy creatures". The first term seems to be used with inaccurate looseness, as Afric's lover is a man old enough to be a diplomat. But this is throughout a flippant and derisory use of the character-type of male homosexual. He is constantly made to seem pathetic and absurd, attempting to marry the heroine in an attempt to alleviate the punishing loneliness which is his unavoidable lot, and being edged out, virtually at the altar, by the handsome (straight) hero.

As an antidote to heartless or hostile treatments, we may turn to the work of Mary Renault. This woman writer, whose reputation has never quite achieved the highest literary reaches, is nevertheless well known to the reading public for her sympathetic and thoughtful studies of male homosexuality. Her special interest lies in the classical world; and in books like *The Last Of The Wine* (1956), *The King Must Die* (1958), and *The Mask Of Apollo* (1966), she has reworked and revitalised different tracts of Greek history and prehistory, each one seen through the perspective of a homosexual love affair. It is arguable that she glamorises and romanticises her subjects, choosing as her protagonists, for example, men of god-like stature or heroic attainment, like Theseus

173

and Alexander the Great. There is, too, a dangerous approxima-
tion to the conventions of Hollywood epic when historical per-
sonages like Alcibiades and Demosthenes casually wander across
the action as extras. And Mary Renault throughout avoids confronting the possibly distasteful reality of any overtly sexual act
by the use of such euphemisms as "sharing a cloak".

Against this, it is evident even from partial and limited evidence
that the Greeks themselves found homosexual love just as capable
of a romantic interpretation as heterosexual, thrilling themselves
with accounts of the heroic demise of the Sacred Band of Thebes,
when homosexual lovers, fighting side by side, the older and
stronger protecting his younger lover, died as one man at the
battle of Chaeronea. These were, even to those living through
them, golden ages of man, and full of superhuman beings and
achievements; and perhaps critics should not cavil at the absence
of any of the more graphic physical details of this type of relationship when standard wisdom decrees that it is the quality
of the feeling, not the physical actions, which denotes love truly.

This is, in fact, a main clue to Mary Renault's angle and
method. Her theme is, essentially, love, which she calls "the most
treacherous word in the language". This phrase, from *The
Charioteer* (1953), characterises one of her rare ventures into a
twentieth-century setting for her homosexual lovers. This is a
Second World War story, in which she tries to trace and account
for the development of an ordinary little boy into an adult who
can love only those of his own sex. Some of the material is quite
rigidly schematised in line with contemporary psychological theoris-
ing on the subject. There is the scene showing the departure
of the central character's father, which ensures that Laurie will
henceforth be brought up as a "mummy's boy". There is the
public school conditioning, the worshipping adoration experienced
for the Head of the House; then, and decisively, the Forces in
wartime. Here Laurie meets and falls in love with a boy whom
he feels is too young to be asked to admit "the love that dare not
speak its name", either on his own or on another's account. While
he is wrestling with this difficulty, his Head of House, now a
bronzed, blue-eyed sea-captain, re-enters his life. The stage is set
for an unorthodox version of the Eternal Triangle.

Unorthodox it may be, but still deeply familiar in its intrinsic qualities. The reader will be fascinated by the closely observed social detail of homosexual domestic life, the flats, the odd parody of womanly housekeeping, the parties, the "marriages", the flirtations and casual pickups. Mary Renault introduces a wide range of men from the calm doctor, Alec, to the nauseous male whore Bunny, in an effort to establish that masculine love breaches all divisions of class, occupation, and educational background in its establishing of a reassuring group, a defence against society. There are some memorable moments which could only have occurred in a homosexual setting, such as the portentous discussion of the situation of homosexuals in relation to "normal" people, which is shattered by a truculent and drunken observation from one of the party that "a lot of bull is talked about Greece by people who'd just have been a dirty laugh there".

But these elements aside, the novel is in essence a romance, a tale about how Laurie triumphed over adversity and found his true love. Like the American Civil War in *Gone With The Wind*, the Dunkirk references serve only to create a colourful backdrop to the love story, in which the condition of being homosexual is just one of those external nuisances which true lovers must reckon on as part of their lot. The novel ends with Laurie united in understanding (though not, as far as we are told, in any other way) with his lover, and settling down to a long and happy life with him as the twilight sinks over the hill. In this alone, the imposition of a conventional happy ending, Mary Renault declares the form within which she is working; and on those terms, hers is a highly unusual and successful book. We should look unjustly and in vain if we sought in it any expression of the authentic plight of the homosexual, like that given such powerful voice in James Baldwin's *Giovanni's Room* (1957) and *Another Country* (1963). It simply isn't that kind of a novel.

If women writers have found it hard to deal genuinely and responsively with male homosexuality, how much more difficult has the subject proved when related to their own sex. (Is this despite, or because of, D. H. Lawrence's belief that consciously or unconsciously, women are nearly all lesbian?) Only one woman writer in this century has seen it as her mission to attempt to tell the truth about women's love for women. Radclyffe Hall established with *The Well Of Loneliness* in 1928 a reputation

THE FICTION OF SEX

which even now has not quite subsided; the present writer discovered that even in 1974 this essentially harmless book is still kept in the reserve stock in several provincial libraries. The book has become, irrespective of literary merits, a classic statement of this theme. In the furore which followed its publication Radclyffe Hall was abused and ostracised, seriously impoverished by the fight through the courts against charges of obscenity, and finally driven from the country as an enemy of young girls, married love, and the stability of the family. Her plea for an increased understanding and tolerance of this deviation was received virtually as an attempt to subvert the state. Such venomous and hysterical reactions are invariably based on a biased or incomplete reading of the work under review. Few people, then or since, took pains really to discover Radclyffe Hall's attitudes or to analyse her work dispassionately.

Had this been done, there might have been some surprise at the result. For it is one of literature's little ironies that the woman writer who is commonly thought of as the voice of female homosexuality should display in her work a sturdier set of traditional sexual stereotypes than most heterosexual authors. Even the writer who set out to reclaim and dignify this aspect of human love, herself a homosexual, could not be free of the countless other pressures which condition behaviour. A study of *A Saturday Life* (1925) shows clearly how Radclyffe Hall's concept of sexuality is modified by her awareness of its function in society. The novel is unmistakably homosexual in theme, tone, and emotional purpose, yet its social and moral values assert the supremacy of the other world. Homosexual feeling is defined and limited by the "normal" emotional modes, and subordinated throughout to them. The norm in this case is that of the independent, conservative middle class among which the action takes place. As a result class emerges as a more significant agent in the definition of personality than sex or sexual behaviour. The satisfaction of class demands, the subtle, stringent exaction of conformity, not only determine the heroine's ultimate fate but precondition each stage of her career.

A Saturday Life tells the story of Sidonia from birth to marriage. She is a difficult child whose management is largely left to Frances, a friend of the family. Her restlessness leads her to experiment with the dance, piano, art, singing, life in Italy, and personal relationships (the novel's rather wilfully obscure title refers to an Eastern belief concerning this sort of dilettante existence). Radclyffe Hall constantly treats Sidonia's course as an emotional pilgrimage of a purely artistic nature. This ignores the truth that it is only made possible by the fact that Sidonia inhabits that social class which can both afford the search for, and expect the reward of, self-fulfilment. Similarly society requires and class describes the final marriage, as Sidonia subsides into a woolly happiness that is highly inartistic but predetermined by the fictional convention that follows the social so closely.

This failure to grasp or even to acknowledge in passing the interaction of the social and personal is related to a certain structural malfunction in the novel. Nominally its heroine is Sidonia, and her growing up provides its subject and framework. But the emotional centre and motive force of the narrative is the homosexual woman, Frances. This character, whose name conveys the first intimation of her intersexuality, Radclyffe Hall projects as the type colloquially called "butch lesbian", or, vulgarly ,"dyke". Her hair is touched at the temples with a "gentlemanly greyness"; she wears an eyeglass, suit, shirt, and tie; she affects a no-nonsense attitude in emotional situations—"You'll find the liver pills in the right-hand corner of the bathroom cupboard, I should take a dose"—or blows her nose gruffly when genuinely moved. She acts as the male partner to the feeble Lady Shore, Sidonia's mother, who literally weeps on her shoulder and turns to her in every crisis. Frances's spiritual retreat is her study, which, with its leather armchairs and ancestral portraits, is furnished to resemble as closely as possible "the smoking room of a Piccadilly club". Here Frances smokes, broods, twiddles her eyeglass, and reflects on the women in her life.

It is clearly stated that Frances never thinks of herself as a woman. With perverse logicality, having cast herself as a man, she assumes the traditional masculine superiority to women. She considers a thousand pounds a year enough for a woman to live on, though her income more than doubles that amount; she thinks in a contemptuous generalisations of "the average woman", "the other female millions", that "God intended them to marry and have nice babies". Clearly Frances is the Radclyffe

177

Hall figure. Her attitudes are her creator's, and this is especially remarkable in the handling of Sidonia's brief infatuation with her. Poised on the brink, this would-be wild adolescent is rather a nympholeptic projection than a real character, created to satisfy the imagination of a raffish but still deeply conformist female homosexual (Radclyffe Hall's self-image emerges from Una Troubridge's *Life And Death of Radclyffe Hall*, 1961, p. 46; her initial pose, "How do I know if I will care for you in six months time?", gave way to a lifelong devotion). Certainly the sequence reads like wish-fulfilment fantasy, employing the tone and vocabulary of standard romance, although with some homosexual colouring. Sidonia is boyish, tall and thin, but lest this seem too austere, the author throws in a hint of fullness and sensuality with "masses of auburn hair" and "huge eyes". In her admiration for Frances, Sidonia is rendered "limp and adoring" like any pulp fiction romantic heroine. Some confusion of sexual roles in this courtship is indicated by Sidonia's opening gambit: "If I were a man I'd marry you, Frances. I'd fall in love with you if you were a man." A further layer of psychic insecurity is revealed when Sidonia adds demanding child to seductive woman as she makes her move proper:

". . . I need someone real, I need *you*! Why can't I have you? Aren't I younger than mother? Aren't I attractive? Don't I interest you enough? Frances"—she began to speak softly now—"Frances, look at me! Don't you love me? Frances, won't you be my friend? I don't want to marry anyone, I tell you; I just want to work, and have you, all of you. . . ." She laid her hand caressingly on Frances's arm. "Frances, why won't you love me?"

(p. 71)

Predictably, nothing comes of this. Frances, a sheep in wolf's clothing, disengages herself "very gently" and leaves. The strangulation of the new love by the old forms, both social and artistic, is soon accomplished. Frances's efforts to find a husband for Sidonia give rise to some predictable man-baiting. All the suitors have weak chins, fishy eyes, and sheepish looks. But when one of more than average bone-headedness presents himself, his more than average wealth and social standing carry the day. Married, this man becomes even more bigoted and overbearing; Frances endures with gritted teeth repeated drenchings as he splashes

178

about in the shallows of his ignorance. The novel ends with the birth of the first child. Frances accepts fairly happily Sidonia's pronouncement as she sums up her varied career and its climax in motherhood, "I've a feeling that it's always ended like this". But our sympathy and interest remain where they have been throughout, with Frances; and there is an unavoidable pathos, both within the terms of the novel and without, in the use of the homosexual woman to further, and finally to glorify, the conventional concept of undistinguished heterosexual romance.

Pathos there is again, and much more, in Radclyffe Hall's major work, *The Well of Loneliness*. This novel makes compulsive reading, despite the flaws of the style, which tends to alternate between the florid and the flat. What gives the novel its horsepower is the massive drive, the obsessive conviction of the writer which is evident in every page. Una Troubridge has related the way in which Radclyffe Hall came to see it almost as a divinely-dictated labour that she should attempt the first full-length and sympathetic study of female homosexuality in fiction. That the novel is very substantially autobiographical makes its revelations even more arresting. It is clear that Radclyffe Hall was not motivated by exhibitionism in this account. The note that is sounded throughout is that of the honest soul's duty to stand up and be counted. Much of the revelation springs from a disgusted refusal to tolerate any longer the hypocritical evasions and self-deceptions of regular members of society. These are the words with which the homosexual heroine of the novel, Stephen Gordon, is heartened to take up her burden of "abnormality" by a sympathiser: ". . . we're all part of nature. Some day the world will recognise this, but meanwhile there's plenty of work that's waiting. For the sake of all the others who are like you, but less strong and less gifted perhaps, many of them, it's up to you to have the courage to make good". It is plain from her life as well as from her work that the writer herself felt much along this line.

And even today, after nearly fifty years, the novel for which she was so reviled and humiliated at the time has lost little of its power to move and to disturb. It relates, with a vivid sense of injury, the various shattering stages by which Stephen is made aware that she is not like other women, and may not expect to live freely in her own mode of existence. She comes to regard her temperament as damned, herself as bearing the mark of Cain, the outcast, and her whole existence as a supernal aberration, "God's mistake". In an era where even "normal" behaviour was fairly rigidly constrained by social and moral rules, such feelings of love as Stephen shyly nourishes are doomed from the start. Consequently her saga is one of inevitable disappointment or betrayal in love, since despite her painful longing to love and be loved in return, Stephen can never believe that she deserves or can retain any affection. She is not surprised that her first lover ruthlessly throws her over when self-interest dictates the move, and offers no reproach, but only the appallingly humble "I'm just a poor, heart-broken freak of a creature who loves you".

Later, she achieves, briefly, a deep and happy relationship with another girl. But she comes to feel that their love, at first mutually delightful, is having a damaging effect upon her lover. She sees Mary's personality coarsening and weakening under the strain of the hothouse lesbian life, cut off from full membership of society. In addition, Stephen begins to be certain that she is depriving Mary, in husband, children, acceptance, security, of more than she can offer her in devoted companionship, comfort, and protection. The more grimly she settles into the acceptance of herself as a "freak", the less is she able to countenance dragging Mary down with her. In an apocalyptic conclusion Stephen nerves herself to kill Mary's love for her and to drive her away. Alone, almost maddened by her anguish, suffering "rockets of pain, burning rockets of pain", Stephen sees armies of advancing shades, the accusing ghosts of all her "sisters", who crowd in on her crying "You dare not disown us!" On their behalf Stephen gasps out a plea for the basic right of survival, "Acknowledge us, oh God, before the whole world. Give us also the right to our existence!"

It is not granted to every generation to find a cause worthy of its talents; and as we must not reprobate every novelist for his or her failure to be Charles Dickens or George Eliot, so we cannot with justice reproach today's writers on sexual themes with their inability to generate anything like this sort of intensity. It is nevertheless indicative of the thinness of recent efforts that the modern fictional heroine makes such heavy weather out of the way of man with maid, while this classic travelogue of the wilder shores of female experience is half a century old and still not reached again, let alone superseded. A survey of the use made of the unprecedented freedom of the last ten years or so suggests that far from being a "liberation" it has become the new tyranny. The inner voyage, the journey of personal exploration was, originally, merely one way of writing fiction; but now, it seems, everyone has to buy a ticket. Let us hope that the more specifically sexual routes will shortly be discontinued. We have surely had enough, for instance, of Up the Uterus, and our guides, those women writers who have given the "lady novelist" tag an entirely new dimension, can no longer pretend that they are leading us into unknown territory. Perhaps a way forward is offered by John Bayley's summary, "Sex is ridiculous. . . . Love is not" (*The Characters of Love*, Chapter 1). If women writers are ever to lend to their treatments of sexuality that experience of balance and calm which we associate with great work, then they will have to look harder outward than in.

7

Sexual Stereotypes and the Image of Woman

I shall move north. I shall move into a long blackness.
I see myself as a shadow, neither man nor woman,
Neither a woman, happy to be like a man, nor a man,
Blunt and flat enough to feel no lack. I feel a lack.
I hold my fingers up, ten white pickets.
See, the darkness is leaking from the cracks.
I cannot contain it. I cannot contain my life.

(Sylvia Plath, *Winter Trees*, 1971)

There was a lady loved a swine,
Honey, quoth she,
Pig-hog wilt thou be mine?
Hoogh, quoth he.

I'll build thee a silver sty,
Honey, quoth she,
And in it thou shalt lie,
Hoogh, quoth he.

Pinned with a silver pin,
Honey, quoth she,
That thou mayst go out and in,
Hoogh, quoth he.

Wilt thou have me now,
Honey? quoth she,
Speak, or my heart will break
Hoogh, quoth he.

(English folk rhyme).

182

"There are only two kinds of women, the plain and the coloured." Twentieth-century fictional developments have given a new slant to Wilde's quip. The highly-coloured revelations of some women writers have made the efforts of others look very dull indeed. What has been the real legacy of the great "breakthrough" of the nineteen-sixties?

First, there has been an increased and distressing tendency to debase the whole issue. Public interest in women writing about their sexuality has led inevitably to exploitation. We have seen a considerable amount of what George Eliot called "authorship on the principle of the gin-palace", giving the public what it wants, however bad it may be. It cannot be interpreted as any advance for women, or for the novel as an art form, that they should adopt the deplorable habit of febrile self-exposure for money, or revive the "female confessional" school of writing which was so prominent an element of Victorian pornography. There is always the danger that this sort of writing, however honestly and "sincerely" intended, will bring both author and subject into deep contempt and disrepute; many still feel with Shakespeare, that "to such as boasting show their scars, a mock is due". What, too, do they or we really gain? John Bayley has warned against the use of absolute frankness as a deeply falsifying impulse and method. Then there are always the commercially-minded who are quite ready to climb up on their sisters' backs to make their impact (and their fortunes). Such women writers as Grace Metallious and Jacqueline Susann, with their grossly vulgarised and degraded accounts of women's sexuality, are merely taking neo-pornographic advantage of freedoms won with all serious purpose by others. These ineffable productions are warmly welcomed and publicised even in the staider of our newspapers. Typical is this breathless example from the *Sunday Times*, February 17, 1974:

> *Fear of Flying*, currently America's top-selling novel, is due out here in April. Billed as Portnoy's Complaint from the female viewpoint, its torrid love scenes are admitted by its author, poetess Erica Jong, to be blatantly autobiographical; the novel, says John Updike, 'wears its gossamer disguise as fiction with breath-taking impudence". And the hottest moment of all comes on the heroine's trip to London, where she shacks up with a Laingian psychoanalyst. . . .

183

A regrettable but inevitable outcome of this whole process was the announcement that the Olympia Press, already well known in the field of sex publishing, is to start a special imprint, Orlando Press, of erotic books for women, written by women. Any profits from this enterprise will accrue to the press's male owner, Maurice Girodias, although an attractive female editor is (of course) placed in charge of the public relations (pubic relations?). When we finally take into account spoof fictions like *I Was Daisy Smuten* and "Rosalind Erskine's" *Passion Flower Hotel* series, where individual or groups of male writers combined to cash in on the reading public's interest in this type of women's writing, then it is a dingy picture indeed of callousness, prurience, want of taste, and simple greed. No liberation here for women.

As a second legacy, the degenerative tendency is present even in serious fiction. The currently marked and even increasing interest in women writers and their subject-matter may look promising, a belated redressing of the historical imbalance. But this has not meant parity of consideration for women. In some cases it has served to deepen the gulf between men and women, and even to disadvantage women further. A feminist critic will not be encouraged by any of the contemporary manifestations of the treatment of sexual themes. It is doubtless to be welcomed that novelists today have greater flexibility in the treatment of unpleasant topics like cancer (note how this has become an important metaphor of modern society in works as different as Kingsley Amis's *The Anti-Death League*, Iris Murdoch's *Bruno's Dream*, and Penelope Mortimer's *My Friend Says It's Bullet-Proof*). But the habit now is not simply to present but to relish the unpleasant, to glorify violence, brutality, and vulgarity. These are seen either as important exercises in their own right for the flexing of the developing male ego, or as necessary and merited forms of masculine relaxation from the strains of life. The more outspoken of these treatments have been celebrated as raising our awareness of a peculiarly contemporary form of sexual unease, and hence, by inference, increasing our understanding of men and women in their sexual roles. But sexual definition in current fiction proceeds, as it has always done, by opposition. The freer, theoretically, males and females have been in the last years to adopt or to emulate each others' behavioural modes, the more tightly have authors clung to defining their characters in terms of extreme versions of the clichés of sex difference. So, many female characters have become increasingly "sensitive" and submissive, while by complementary interaction males are drawn into action and aggression.

This point is made with excruciating precision by Philip Roth in his brilliant *Portnoy's Complaint* (1967). Whatever the precise nature of Portnoy's complex condition, among his drives is certainly the need continually to test his concept of manhood along with other misleading and inadequate notions of behaviour which he has inherited from his culture. His heroically unflagging attempts to define himself through the pursuit of "pussy" are both symptom and illness; the cure will fail because the cause continues to flourish. Portnoy's confusion, we are told, is rooted in his mother's determination to turn him into the type of male most acceptable to a Jewish mother. But all he learns at his mother's knee is an acute antifeminism. The constant urging to be a good Jewish boy produces a bad Jewish boy, perpetually fixated in the "badness" of boyhood, pathologically unable to grow up. His suffering is produced by his awareness of his situation, and by the tension between his drive to be a man and his dissatisfaction with the sort of man he has to be; or, rather, his dissatisfaction with traditional methods of demonstrating manhood, the meaningless rites of masturbation and copulation.

Portnoy's feelings of desperation escalate into frenzy. He is impelled into reckless and savage acts of sexual aggression, which do not relieve but restore and renew the tensions of his failure. Here he decides to give venereal disease to a kibbutz girl whom he has met on holiday in Israel, because she has refused, not surprisingly, to take seriously his offers of love and marriage.

> "Oh, I am going to fuck you, Jew girl," I whispered evilly . . . "you have got a lesson to learn, Naomi," and pressed, pressed hard, to teach my lesson: O you virtuous Jewess, the tables are turned, *tsatskeleh*! *You* on the defensive now, Naomi—explaining your vaginal discharge to the entire kibbutz. Wait'll they get a whiff of this! . . . Then perhaps you'll come to have the proper awe for us fallen psychoneurotic Jewish men! Socialism exists, but so do spirochetes, my love! So here's your introduction, dear, to the slimier side of things. Down, down with those patriotic khaki

shorts, spread your chops, blood of my blood, unlock your fortressy thighs, open wide that messianic Jewish hole! Make ready, Naomi, I am about to poison your organs of reproduction! I am about to change the future of the race!

But of course I couldn't. Licked her earholes, sucked at her un-washed neck, sank my teeth into the coiled braids of hair . . . and then, even as resistance may actually have begun to recede under my assault, I rolled off her and came to rest, defeated, against the wall—on my back. "It's no good," I said "I can't get a hard-on in this place."

("In Exile")

It is significant that physical failure, not moral scruple, is all that prevents him. Portnoy simply cannot feel for women other than as lust objects. They do not have the reality of humanity in his eyes. He sets out, with unselfconscious directness, his idea of sex: "What I'm saying, Doctor, is that I don't seem to stick my dick up these girls, as much as I stick it up their back-grounds—as though through fucking I will discover America. *Conquer* America—maybe that's more like it." He also uses incidental women, in his travels through "the cunt in country-'tis-of-thee", to pay off scores inflicted by men of their social class, though through no fault of theirs, on his own family. He sums up his affair with a girl from a good background in these words; Sarah Abbot Maulsby "was just something nice a son once did for his dad. A little vengeance on Mr Lindabury for all those nights and Sundays Jack Portnoy spent collecting down in the coloured district. A little bonus extracted from Boston and Northeastern, for all those years of service, and exploitation." Pity the chop-logic which compensates for one form of exploitation with another; and pity the ignorant, trusting Sarah, too. What price any love, affection, respect for the individual when each encounter is a cold grinding of the axe of resentment and rage?

Portnoy is of course a comic novel, often side-splittingly funny and, in its fertility of wit and invention, sheer joy to read. Many would feel that to analyse it in this way is to take it too seriously. Norman Mailer has similarly complained that women critics of Henry Miller fail to see that Miller is "only" being humorous, that he does not intend his sexual scenarios with their use and abuse of women to be taken too earnestly. Mailer in his turn fails to perceive that this is precisely what women are objecting to, that the joke is, quite literally in some cases, on them. Women are only just beginning to realise that male humour has various functions, but none of them is intended to please or benefit them. It can be a bonding device, assisting male solidarity (and excluding women). It can be a smoke-screen, set up to dissipate an aura of good humour (distracting and deceiving women). Finally, it can be a form of assault, a teasing attack (putting women in that mythical region, their place). In any event it is used to avoid, to impede, or to deride the possibility of free equal relationships between men and women. That is how it is used in Mailer, Miller, and Roth. And that is what some women feel that they don't have to put up with any longer.

Henry Miller is now passé, his faded dreams superseded by works that make his trailblazing efforts seem tame. But where one ageing comedian quits the stage, there is always another with a great sense of humour waiting in the wings. The contemporary obsession with tough masculinity, with sexual aggression and physical prowess as a means of defining manhood is nowhere more clearly expressed than in Anthony Burgess's *A Clockwork Orange* (1962). This novel, although puffed as one big laugh, "horror farce", is clearly nothing so lighthearted. It is, for all its humour, to those who can see it, a sermon on the dangers of the cult of brutalism in modern England.

The hero, Alex, is first presented to the reader as an expert practitioner in the art of "sheer wantonness and vandalwork", not to mention grievous bodily harm and sexual assault. Physically he is fully mature, indeed accomplished enough to take on two of his "droogs" armed with knife and chain, and defeat them. So implicitly do we accept these manifestations of adult manhood that it strikes with some effect of horror when Burgess reveals half way through the novel that Alex is only fifteen. Yet if fifteen seems not to be his physical age, it is even more discrepant with his emotional age. His is not the painful stirring consciousness of adolescence, but the total clarity and overwhelming ego of the child. He exerts his male power in a moral void, a man in all but the one controlling factor, the sense of others.

The novel also brings out the latent violence and hostility to

THE FICTION OF SEX

women which is implicit in the cult of bullhood. This passage links the act of destruction with that of sex as temporary outlets for Alex's brutality and aggression. The negative drive of his purpose, rape and mayhem, is startlingly contrasted with the vital creativity of the prose, his own special language, in which he relates it:

"All right, Dim," I said. "Now for the other veshch, Bog help us all." So he did the strong-man on the devotchka, who was still creech creech creeching away in very horrorshow four-in-a-bar, locking her rookers from the back, while I ripped away at this and that and the other, the others going haw haw haw still, and real good horrorshow groodies they were that then exhibitee their pink glazzies, O my brothers, while I untrussed and got ready for the plunge. Plunging, I could slooshy cries of agony and this bleeding writer veck that Georgie and Pete held on to nearly got loose howling bezoomny with the filthiest of slovos that I already knew and others he was making up. Then after me it was right old Dim should have his turn, which he did in a beastly snorty howly sort of a way with his Peebee Shelley maskie taking no notice, while I held on to her. Then there was a changeover, Dim and me grabbing on to the slobbering writer veck who was past struggling really, only just coming out with slack sort of slovos like he was in the land in a milk-plus bar, and Pete and Georgie had theirs. Then there was like quiet and we were full of like hate, so smashed what was left to be smashed—typewriter, lamp, chairs— and Dim, it was typical of old Dim, watered the fire out and was going to dung on the carpet, there being plenty of paper, but I said no. "Out out out out" I howled. The writer veck and his zheena were not really there, bloody and torn and making noises. But they'd live.

So we got into the waiting auto and I left it to Georgie to take the wheel, me feeling that malenky bit shagged, and we went back to town, running over odd squealing things on the way.

(Chapter Two)

"Odd squealing things"—this phrase could sum up many women writers and their characters today. The relegation of women to the most basic functional level, the use of them as outlets for masculine problems or tensions, is hardly new— Sonya Tolstoy came to see herself, with extreme bitterness, as "a vase". But it may well be that ours is the first generation to be made conscious of it in so widespread and brutal a way. What is disturbing is not that individual males are shown to have these assumptions, but that women are so weakly inclined to accept this poor estimate of themselves. Masculine hostility, internalised, becomes masochism of a most lowering kind; it works insidiously in the female imagination to confirm belief in the repugnant nature of women and women's sexuality. We have seen how the hypergamous husband or demon lover continues to weave his ancient way through modern fiction, often to cries of female delight all round; we should now take account of some of the damage he causes on his endless missions of search and destroy:

> I remembered Nelson telling me how sometimes he looked at his wife's body and hated it for its femaleness; he hated it because of the hair in the armpits and around the crotch. Sometimes, he said, he saw his wife as a sort of spider, all clutching arms and legs around a hairy central devouring mouth. I sat on my bed and I looked at my thin white legs and thin white arms, and at my breasts. My wet sticky centre seemed disgusting, and when I saw my breasts all I could think of was how they were when they were full of milk, and instead of this being pleasurable, it was revolting.
>
> (*The Golden Notebook*, p. 524)

We have already looked at some of the sexual problems of Doris Lessing's Anna; and it is clear that not unlike Fanny Price in *Mansfield Park* she suffers from a condition of debility in which a generally low self-esteem is frequently experienced through sharp feelings of sexual inadequacy. Anna, however, receives no authorial tonic like that with which Jane Austen perks up her heroine for the final settlement. On the contrary, she is presented as going through a difficult and painful phase of life— we cannot say crisis, since this suggests a finite episode, which is quite at variance with the tone and structure of the book— whose developments as they occur force her to turn in on herself more and more. From the outset a somewhat taut and wary creature, Anna becomes progressively more constricted; but her anxiety over her mental state and her desire to change it cannot make her effective. Since she is the prisoner of a deep and humiliating dependence upon men—better a tame homosexual to share her flat than no man at all—this very factor leads her to take on males irrespective of their reliability or kindness. Successive failures then lead her to internalise what she comes to see as inevitable, the eventual male rejection of the female. We see in this passage Anna's lowest moment in the novel, when she is reduced to a condition which is almost a parody of female inertia and masochism.

These then are studies of the new man and the new woman of our time, the new sexual stereotypes of twentieth-century fiction. The slow violence of the resulting distortion from basic human values leads inevitably to neurosis. Portnoy, Alex, and Anna are deeply disturbed, and part of the quality of the novels in which they appear derives from their authors' ability to create for us the exact rhythms of their obsessions. Doris Lessing finishes with Anna not unhopefully. The turning to *The Golden Notebook* at the end, with the revelation that what we have been reading is what it contained, brings some sense of light and movement (even if circular) into the conclusion. Alex, too, is "rehabilitated", though hardly in the way that we expect. But Portnoy is brought to the edge and over; we are left with his scream as he plunges down. The novel's last line, with its inevitable echo of Sartre's *Huis Clos*, consigns him finally to the modern version of Purgatory, the process of psychoanalysis: "So [said the Doctor]. Now vee may perhaps to begin. Yes?" This line tells us that the Doctor to whom Portnoy has been speaking all the way through has not heard or regarded his narrative; and we, since we too have been present all the way through, are by extension implicated in this failure, almost even become the heedless doctor, neglectful of the desperate need of a fellow man. This, Roth's final irony in a piece layered with ironic significances, is a quelling reminder of our own inadequacy, our own "sickness".

In such ways as these are men and women degraded by modern "values" in sex relationships. Is it surprising that the retreat from the front line of the sex war, where females are injured or weakened by male hostility, is in full flow, that women are still making romances for themselves and their readers, to console and distract them among the comforting conventional material of everyday life? There are times when it seems, to judge from the fiction of the last few years, that women's emancipation from social trivialities and petty issues is farther away than ever. The

greater the educational opportunities, the greater the ease of movement in a less overtly restricted society, the greater the number of
areas in which women have to compete with each other. If an
American experience has any wider validity, consider this account,
by Beverley Gasner, of an attractive college girl's view of her
duller schoolmate:

> Don't be sorry for mousy girls, Marina instructed herself, meanly;
> they all turn into rats eventually. Marriage does the job, the man,
> children, eighteen of monogrammed everything. The mouse puts
> on muscle; now she can put other people in their places. For
> example, she can say to her zero mouse-mate, Let's not have the
> Yoo-hoos this time; she's such a pill. And the male loser says
> happily, Sure, leave 'em out, who needs 'em because he, too, must
> have some old scores to settle, or why did he marry a mouse in
> the first place?

(Girls' Rules, 1969, p. 6)

The character of Marina, as drawn, is not that of an habitually
unkind or dismissive girl. But she is rendered negative, and hence
destructive, by the gulf that she perceives between her personal
standards and society's expectations. She is too critical to make
the sort of marriage which she sees her friends all around settling
down to, marriage which simply intensifies in its participants their
worst and most antisocial characteristics—"mice" become "rats".
We sympathise with her contempt for the vacuity of the ostenta-
tion ("monogrammed everything"), and feel that she correctly
disdains both the socialite hostess and the identikit guests the
Yoo-hoos (Yahoos?).

Yet the passage is acute with jealousy and the longing for what
is censured. It seems desirable to be able to "put other people
in their places"; it assumes that one has a place of one's own
from which to operate the social mechanisms of condescension.
For Marina's education, and her bachelor graduate life in New
York, have not freed her from even the most basic dictates of a
capitalistic social structure, whose workings she glimpses as she
suffers from, but whose decrees form a series of inescapable abso-
lutes for her. All her thinking is debased by assumptions of competition and acquisition. She automatically reduces the less lively
girl to the sub-human level of "mouse", and stamps on the
temptation to feel pity for this creature on the grounds that

191

she will turn, not eventually into a human being like herself (for this is the unacknowledged thought), but into a rat, an enemy and super-competitor. Released and empowered, the mouse demonstrates how well it has learned the lessons of aggression and competition; and herself a victim of the same syndrome Marina never questions that this must always happen. Finally she judges the male partner by these values—he is a loser by definition if he is married, and so such a specimen—yet paradoxically even he in his inferiority can convey the sacred status; "marriage", the bland social imperative, "does the job". This crude phrase is used to indicate both Marina's contempt and her desperation. The only defence she can muster for her beleaguered ego is the petty sartorial revenge: "Celia ought to know that big high collars and short necks do not belong together." Here, if we have not already recognised it as such, is a directive from the world of women's magazines, those immensely powerful shapers of attitudes and creators of values which in every way reflect and regulate the consumer nightmare which is Marina's existence.

It would be good to think that Beverley Gasner is being satirical. In a sense, she is; many gibes are directed at those who fail to measure up. But the ultimate standard remains the social, or rather, she does not achieve that level of satiric comment at which social and moral fuse. Her characters, like those of so many women writers, fail the test not through foolishness or corruption, but through cheap boots, faded suntans, ill-fitting clothes, and too much or too little bosom. *Girls' Rules* has some fine and perceptive moments, which this summary does not consider, but it betrays throughout a central fault of much women's writing, even the best, that faith in the glamour of position and exhibition which is an essential constituent of "romance".

Nearer home, we have the modern novel which makes a romance of "trendiness"; this too leaves women, as characters, washed up and washed out. Stories like A. S. Byatt's *The Game* (1967) and her sister Margaret Drabble's *The Needle's Eye* (1972), with their casts of journalists, telly "personalities", *au pair* girls, and novel-writing ladies, evoke a world of colour-supplement superficiality and meaningless behaviour. In such a setting the women are naturally characterised by a childish acquisitiveness and pride of possession, whether it be of money, things, publications, or sexual conquests. The increasing use of the world of communications—television, journalism, advertising—as something attractive and desirable, has become a thumping cliché of the modern novel.

Were it one great yawn only, that would be bad enough. But this historical process threatens seriously to impoverish our ideas of what is exciting, glamorous, and worth sighing for; what is *romantic*, in short. Thus, in Elizabeth Jenkins' portrait of the "fashionable" magazine writer, Magda, in *Honey*, we are told that although "intellectual", successful, well-off and talented, what she "secretly wanted more than anything else" was sexual success. Apart from the belittling conception of woman's nature implied here (remember "Love is of man's life a thing apart/'Tis woman's whole existence"?), it is pathetic that "sexual success" is thought of as a glamorous thing in itself, by itself—not as success with the desired and desirable Rodolphe, say. Certainly in the Emma Bovary prototype there is an inextricable connection between sex, romance, and glamour; but nowadays, the more sex, the less glamour; and modern writers have not yet been entirely successful in their endeavours to convince us all of the romance of copulation.

That other fictional modes than these are available to women writers goes without saying. Compare the contrasted use of the "I" narrator made by Doris Lessing and Iris Murdoch. Murdoch uses this in *A Severed Head* (1961), experimentally, one feels, in order to see how many surprises she can spring on the reader through his naïve assumption that the first-person narrator sees all that is to be seen, and tells us the truth about it. She also clearly enjoys giving the narrator himself some unexpected blows —indeed, this is part of his education in the novel—since he is a self-absorbed and hypochondriacal male of a type much in need of some readjustment. Doris Lessing's "I" on the other hand, is a female voice crying in the wilderness, insisting on the centrality of being a woman, which for Iris Murdoch is only one of several levels of human validity. When the heroine-narrator is, as here, characterised by a limited existence, limited means, both financial and emotional, a limited circle, and ultimately by a limited projection even of what she understands by "being a woman", then it is not surprising that this study does not approach the effortless generalisation which is Iris Murdoch's forte.

This wonderful writer offers in her work a wide variety of female types, lover, wife, child-woman, and servant. Her weakness is that she cannot quite give us the *individual* on each occasion; we feel we know the type, but not the person. It is probable though, that she turns this into a strength; she may not be acute on character, but she is faultless in her summation and presentation of women in their social roles, and also in their mythic capacities. Lessing shows Anna's perceiving other women in relation to herself; Murdoch, with the "shifting centre of interest" technique, concentrates on bringing out the pattern. These two methods are not to be regarded competitively, but only comparatively, in order to illustrate the range of methods available to women writers, a range that some of them have sacrificed in their concentration on female experience.

Interestingly enough, it was Doris Lessing who herself in 1971 took her way out of the Ladies' Room of the modern novel. *Briefing For A Descent Into Hell* she describes as "inner space fiction", but the novel has a wide applicability which is somewhat belied by this title. Her theme is that madness, today, is the only form of sanity; and this is a logical extension of her previous work with its attack upon the norm and the stresses that it imposes on the individual. As *The Golden Notebook* dealt with the sadness of separation from love, so here Lessing hammers away at what she sees as a great loss in modern life: "Some sort of divorce there has been somewhere along the long path of this race of man between the 'I' and the 'We', some sort of terrible falling away". In this work of extreme technical complexity, with its formal blending of stream of consciousness passages with letters, papers, hospital reports, snatches of poetry and narrative, Doris Lessing achieves an almost godlike distance from her material together with an equally divine disgust which lends an impressive authority to her denunciation of human selfishness and separateness:

> To celestial eyes, seen like a broth of microbes under a microscope, always at war and destruction, this scum of microbes thinks, it can see itself, it begins slowly to sense itself as one, a function, a note in the harmony, and this *is* its point and

function, and where the scummy film transcends itself, here and here only and never where these mad microbes say I, I, I, I, I, for saying I, I, I, I, is their madness, this is where they have been struck lunatic, made moonmad, round the bend, crazy, for these microbes are a whole, they form a unity, they have a single mind, a single being, and never can they say I, I, without making the celestial watchers roll with laughter or weep with pity.

(pp. 102–3)

This superbly exciting novel, as challenging stylistically as it is in form, content, and attitude, is the more to be welcomed as it steers clear of those female distresses and difficulties which Doris Lessing seemed to be making her own. Throughout it she urges that we should look outward towards others, not inwards to loneliness and despair; selfishness she sees as the modern madness, and the realisation of our common humanity as the one true task of our lives. This is encouraging not only in regard to this author, but in terms of women's fiction at large.

For Doris Lessing illustrates here the choice which still confronts women writers today. They can tend towards the "masculine" objective fictional stance of George Eliot, assisting the reader to understand and come to terms with his place in the world at large, and with his fellow human beings, seeing the management of life as a *moral* question. Alternatively they can follow the "feminine" subjective novel tradition as it has come down from the nineteenth century in the work of Jane Austen and the Brontës; this invites concentration upon manners and women's conduct in the social and domestic sphere, finding its primary imperative in *emotional* fulfilment and self-discovery.

Each of these modes has its own special drawbacks. Adopting the first may lead simply to the fossilising of outmoded fictional forms, preserving them into an age where they are no longer relevant, and where they serve only to feed the nostalgia of the older reader. It may seem, too, as the "masculine" form, to be inimical to the particular needs and qualities of women's writing; it cannot express or contain any attempt to write "as a woman".

But of the two, the "feminine" is the fictional mode which has proved, in the long run, to be the more damaging to women's interests. The form which should have freed women to be themselves has, in some cases, merely confined them more closely to a ghetto of their own making. The examination of women as separate and different from men, the recognition of their own peculiar emotional processes and sensibilities, has led at times to an inability or refusal to see women in any other terms than these. This has been responsible for two apparently unrelated modern phenomena, the exaltation of "romance", and the sensational investigation of women's "femininity" which concentrates entirely upon their sexuality.

Taken simply as women, rather than in relation to men and to society as in nineteenth-century fiction, women today have been exploited and self-exploited. The stress upon women's sexuality has in some cases become a way of obscuring or denying their full humanity. While their rational, creative, or administrative skills go largely unremarked, people are making money out of the partial and degraded representation of women as sexual creatures and sex objects. This derogation of women is further accomplished in the contemporary cult of brutalism, with its vaunting of masculine aggression, hostility, and violence. When women writers acquiesce in this disparagement of their sex, or lend themselves to lowering it further, then the result is particularly depressing. It is admittedly the artist's duty to know himself before he can know anything else. But women writers must, as Doris Lessing has, learn to look outside rather than in.

For there is much to be done that only they can do, in the recognition and weeding out of some rubbishy notions, in the readjustment, where possible, of the historical bias against women. As long as the accepted mode of society remains masculine in its orientation, then the general consciousness will continue to be influenced by attitudes inherited from the pursuit of two world wars and the quite unchanged possession by males of property, authority, and power. In this situation the position of women, both as subjects and authors of fiction, will inevitably be "special" and anomalous, if not actually disadvantaged. It is significant that even in the most futuristic avenues of the so-called "apocalyptic" novel in America of John Barth and Thomas Pynchon, or in that odd sport of fiction, the sci-fi novel, there is no real advance posited for the female of the species. Writers who blow their minds dreaming up horrendous changes affecting total environment, technology, and personality, still see change as affecting every area of experience other than this one. Female characters meander through the unimaginable timescapes of the future, still "emotional", still in need of masculine domination, and still unable even to understand the internal combustion engine or to use a screwdriver.

To work against this will be their task as women. They have also their duty to themselves as writers. It seems that they must learn to avoid the specifically female, as George Eliot did. As creative artists they must endeavour to widen their field of vision and experience, not narrow the focus so that only one limited area comes into view. It is only by developing a sense of others, and of the ways in which individuals interact within society, that women writers will be able to free themselves and their sisters from the constrictions of sex-typing and sex-based writing in general. This emancipation will never be achieved by a narrow concentration upon the minutiae of women's lives, the emphasis on domestic difficulties and sexual sorrows. The sheer parochialism of much women's writing today must sound its deathknell; to take an admonition from a writer who succeeded in the artistic obligation to turn personal preoccupations into universal truths, Dostoevsky: "Arid observations of everyday trivialities I have long ceased to regard as realism—it is quite the reverse."

To go outward; to develop a sense of community; to look to the moral rather than to the emotional dimension; to make the right choice and to make it work; these are not only the tasks of women, but of all writers. We should perhaps recall, very clearly, that it is the duty of the novel to be novel—that is, to keep up with, to record, and to comment upon the contemporary. The trials of modern life are very specialised. Our age, with its increased social, educational, and emotional mobility has seen many casualties, and not all female; who would say which of the sexes has felt more acutely the difficulty of the marriage choice, for instance, with all that it implies of established identity, fixed place of residence, constraints upon freedom, and so on? We have come, too, to a fuller acquaintance with the problems of internal migration, awkward transitions of personality which may ruin formerly stable relationships or at best render them obsolete. We have needed our fiction-makers to observe and relate all this, to give a name to every one of the processes of alienation

197

which permeate personality and destroy the capacity for warm and secure loving.

This need becomes more urgent every day as the strains of urban life and a runaway technology bite more deeply. But the challenges of modern fiction to watch, shape up, and recount all this for those of us who are living through it, must be faced in a forward-thinking way. Much previously necessary assimilation in fiction of the disruptive events of life itself has now become outmoded. So, too, have some of the techniques whereby this is carried out, the use of sexual stereotypes and the clichés of sex definition. Every time that a writer capitalises on or even connives at the transmission of these clichés, then he or she is ensuring their perpetuation. For the novel does not only reflect and record experience; it defines and delineates it too. Writers need to be constantly on the alert for the dangerous encroachments of these belittling assumptions, must resist the temptation of the creeping suggestive generalisation. The use of these will not only betray their own limitations, but may be responsible for the imposition of limitations upon others. Twentieth-century fiction must make an effort to shake off the rags and tatters of nineteenth-century thinking which hang about it still. It should seek to assist psychology and sociology in their discovering and developing ways for human beings to live together, free and equal. Then, and only then, will we have the novel that will make "woman's novel" a fatuous and superannuated phrase.

Select Bibliography

All books are published in London, unless otherwise stated.

Appignanesi, Lisa. *Femininity and the Creative Imagination: A Study of Henry James, Robert Musil and Marcel Proust* (1973).
Allott, Miriam K. *Novelists on the Novel* (1959).
Austen-Leigh, James. *Memoir of Jane Austen* (1870).

Bayley, John. *The Characters of Love: A Study in the Literature of Personality* (1960).
Bald, Marjory. *Women-Writers of the Nineteenth Century* (Cambridge, 1923).
Bell, Quentin. *Virginia Woolf, a Biography* (2 vols., 1972).
Bennett, Joan. *Virginia Woolf, Her Art as a Novelist* (Cambridge, 1945).
Bergonzi, Bernard. *The Situation of the Novel* (1970).
Burgess, Anthony. *The Novel Now* (1967).
Byatt, A. S. *Degrees of Freedom* (1965).

Colby, Vineta. *The Singular Anomaly: Women Novelists of the Nineteenth Century* (New York and London, 1970).
Courtney, W. L. *The Feminine Note in Fiction* (1904).
Cox, C. B. *The Free Spirit* (Oxford, 1963).

Daiches, David. *Virginia Woolf* (1945).
Dick, Kay. *Ivy and Stevie* (1971).

Edel, Leon. *The Psychological Novel 1900–1950* (1955).
Egan, Michael. *Henry James: The Ibsen Years* (1972).
Ellis, Havelock. *The Revaluation of Obscenity* (1931).
Ellis, Sarah Stickney. *The Women of England: Their social duties and domestic habits* (1839).

199

Ellman, Mary. *Thinking about Women* (1968).
Ewbank, Inga-Stina. *Their Proper Sphere: A Study of the Brontë Sisters as Early-Victorian Female Novelists* (1966).

Friedan, Betty. *The Feminine Mystique* (1963).

Gray, Nigel. *The Silent Majority: A Study of the Working Class in Post-War British Fiction* (1973).
Greer, Germaine. *The Female Eunuch* (1970).

Johnson, R. Brimley. *Some Contemporary Novelists (Women)* (1920).
Jones, Ernest. *Sigmund Freud: Life and Work* (3 vols., 1953–7).
Jones, Phyllis M. (ed.). *English Critical Essays, Twentieth Century* (1933).

Kermode, Frank. *Lawrence* (1973).
Kroeber, Karl. *Styles in Fictional Structure* (Princeton, 1971).

L.M. *Katherine Mansfield: the Memories of L.M.* (1971).

McCarthy, Mary. *On the Contrary* (1962).
Mailer, Norman. *Cannibals and Christians* (1967).
—— *The Prisoner of Sex* (1971).
Mantz, Ruth Elvish. *The Critical Bibliography of Katherine Mansfield* (1931).
Masefield, Muriel. *Women Novelists from Fanny Burney to George Eliot* (1934).
Mews, Hazel. *Frail Vessels: Women's Role in Women's Novels from Fanny Burney to George Eliot* (1969).
Milford, Nancy. *Zelda Fitzgerald: A Biography* (1970).
Millett, Kate. *Sexual Politics* (1971).
Morgan, Elaine. *The Descent of Woman* (1972).
Murdoch, Iris. *The Sovereignty of Good* (1970).
Murry, John Middleton (ed.). *Katherine Mansfield's Letters to John Middleton Murry: 1913–1922* (1951).
—— *Journal of Katherine Mansfield* (1954).

Nicholson, Nigel. *Portrait of a Marriage* (1973).

Rogers, Katharine M. *The Troublesome Helpmate: A History of Misogyny in Literature* (Seattle and London, 1966).
Ruskin, John. *Ethics of the Dust* (1866).

Savage, D. S. *The Withered Branch: Six Studies in the Modern Novel* (1950).

Schorer, Mark. *The World We Imagine* (1969).

Schreiner, Olive. *Woman and Labour* (1911).

Sprigge, Elizabeth. *The Life of Ivy Compton-Burnett* (1973).

Troubridge, Lady Una. *The Life and Death of Radclyffe Hall* (1961).

Wise, T. J. and Symington, J. A. *The Brontës: Their Lives, Friendships and Correspondences* (4 vols., Oxford, 1932).

Woolf, Leonard (ed.). *A Writer's Diary* (1952).

Woolf, Virginia. *The Common Reader* (1925).

—— *The Death of the Moth* (1942).

—— *A Room of One's Own* (1929).

—— *Three Guineas* (1938).

Index